S0-BYK-318

Just The

facts101
Textbook Key Facts

Textbook Outlines, Highlights, and Practice Quizzes

Criminal Justice: A Brief Introduction

by Frank J. Schmalleger, 10th Edition

All "Just the Facts101" Material Written or Prepared by Cram101 Publishing

Title Page

Visit Cram101.com for full Practice Exams

WHY STOP HERE... THERE'S MORE ONLINE

With technology and experience, we've developed tools that make studying easier and efficient. Like this Cram101 textbook notebook, **Cram101.com** offers you the highlights from every chapter of your actual textbook. However, unlike this notebook, **Cram101.com** gives you practice tests for each of the chapters. You also get access to in-depth reference material for writing essays and papers.

By purchasing this book, you get 50% off the normal subscription free!. Just enter the promotional code **'DK73DW23017'** on the Cram101.com registration screen.

CRAMI0I.COM FEATURES:

Outlines & Highlights
Just like the ones in this notebook, but with links to additional information.

Integrated Note Taking
Add your class notes to the Cram101 notes, print them and maximize your study time.

Problem Solving
Step-by-step walk throughs for math, stats and other disciplines.

Practice Exams
Five different test taking formats for every chapter.

Easy Access
Study any of your books, on any computer, anywhere.

Unlimited Textbooks
All the features above for virtually all your textbooks, just add them to your account at no additional cost.

Be sure to use the promo code above when registering on Cram101.com to get 50% off your membership fees.

Visit Cram101.com for full Practice Exams

STUDYING MADE EASY

This Cram101 notebook is designed to make studying easier and increase your comprehension of the textbook material. Instead of starting with a blank notebook and trying to write down everything discussed in class lectures, you can use this Cram101 textbook notebook and annotate your notes along with the lecture.

Our goal is to give you the best tools for success.

For a supreme understanding of the course, pair your notebook with our online tools. Should you decide you prefer Cram101.com as your study tool,

we'd like to offer you a trade...

Our Trade In program is a simple way for us to keep our promise and provide you the best studying tools, regardless of where you purchased your Cram101 textbook notebook. As long as your notebook is in *Like New Condition**, you can send it back to us and we will immediately give you a Cram101.com account free for 120 days!

Let The **Trade In** Begin!

THREE SIMPLE STEPS TO TRADE:

1. Go to www.cram101.com/tradein and fill out the packing slip information.

2. Submit and print the packing slip and mail it in with your Cram101 textbook notebook.

3. Activate your account after you receive your email confirmation.

* Books must be returned in *Like New Condition*, meaning there is no damage to the book including, but not limited to; ripped or torn pages, markings or writing on pages, or folded / creased pages. Upon receiving the book, Cram101 will inspect it and reserves the right to terminate your free Cram101.com account and return your textbook notebook at the owners expense.

Visit Cram101.com for full Practice Exams

"Just the Facts101" is a Cram101 publication and tool designed to give you all the facts from your textbooks. Visit Cram101.com for the full practice test for each of your chapters for virtually any of your textbooks.

Cram101 has built custom study tools specific to your textbook. We provide all of the factual testable information and unlike traditional study guides, we will never send you back to your textbook for more information.

YOU WILL NEVER HAVE TO HIGHLIGHT A BOOK AGAIN!

Cram101 StudyGuides

All of the information in this StudyGuide is written specifically for your textbook. We include the key terms, places, people, and concepts... the information you can expect on your next exam!

Want to take a practice test?

Throughout each chapter of this StudyGuide you will find links to cram101.com where you can select specific chapters to take a complete test on, or you can subscribe and get practice tests for up to 12 of your textbooks, along with other exclusive cram101.com tools like problem solving labs and reference libraries.

Cram101.com

Only cram101.com gives you the outlines, highlights, and PRACTICE TESTS specific to your textbook. Cram101.com is an online application where you'll discover study tools designed to make the most of your limited study time.

By purchasing this book, you get 50% off the normal monthly subscription fee!. Just enter the promotional code **'DK73DW23017'** on the Cram101.com registration screen.

www.Cram101.com

Copyright © 2013 by Cram101, Inc. All rights reserved.

"Just the FACTS101"®, "Cram101"® and "Never Highlight a Book Again!"® are registered trademarks of Cram101, Inc. ISBN(s): 9781490244037. PUBX-8.2013914

Criminal Justice: A Brief Introduction
Frank J. Schmalleger, 10th

CONTENTS

1. What Is Criminal Justice?

CHAPTER OUTLINE: KEY TERMS, PEOPLE, PLACES, CONCEPTS

	Criminal justice
	Mortgage fraud
	Speedy trial
	Law enforcement
	Emergency management
	Federal Emergency Management Agency
	Witness protection
	Ponzi scheme
	Sarbanes-Oxley Act
	Corporate crime
	White-collar crime
	Sex Offender
	Community policing
	Christopher Commission
	Social justice
	Computer fraud
	CrimeStat
	Fraud
	Domestic violence
	Crime control
	Due process

1. What Is Criminal Justice?

_____ Social control _____

_____ Criminology _____

_____ CAN-SPAM Act _____

_____ Probation _____

_____ Multiculturalism _____

CHAPTER HIGHLIGHTS & NOTES: KEY TERMS, PEOPLE, PLACES, CONCEPTS

Criminal justice	Criminal justice is the system of practices and institutions of governments directed at upholding social control, deterring and mitigating crime, or sanctioning those who violate laws with criminal penalties and rehabilitation efforts. Those accused of crime have protections against abuse of investigatory and prosecution powers. Goals In the United States, criminal justice policy has been guided by the 1967 President's Commission on Law Enforcement and Administration of Justice, which issued a ground-breaking report 'The Challenge of Crime in a Free Society'.
Mortgage fraud	Mortgage fraud is a crime in which the intent is to materially misrepresent or omit information on a mortgage loan application to obtain a loan or to obtain a larger loan than would have been obtained had the lender or borrower known the truth. In United States federal courts, mortgage fraud is prosecuted as wire fraud, bank fraud, mail fraud and money laundering, with penalties of up to thirty years imprisonment. As the incidence of mortgage fraud has risen over the past few years, states have also begun to enact their own penalties for mortgage fraud.
Speedy trial	The Speedy Trial Clause of the Sixth Amendment to the United States Constitution provides that '[i]n all criminal prosecutions, the accused shall enjoy the right to a speedy . . . trial . . . .' The Clause protects the defendant from delay between the presentation of the indictment or similar charging instrument and the beginning of trial.

Law enforcement	Law enforcement broadly refers to any system by which some members of society act in an organized manner to promote adherence to the law by discovering and punishing persons who violate the rules and norms governing that society. Although the term may encompass entities such as courts and prisons, it is most frequently applied to those who directly engage in patrols or surveillance to dissuade and discover criminal activity, and those who investigate crimes and apprehend offenders. Furthermore, although law enforcement may be most concerned with the prevention and punishment of crimes, organizations exist to discourage a wide variety of non-criminal violations of rules and norms, effected through the imposition of less severe consequences.
Emergency management	Emergency management is a public authority field, a group of professions and an interdisciplinary research field that deals with the processes used to protect a population or organization from the consequences of disasters, wars and acts of terrorism. Emergency management doesn't necessarily extend to the averting or eliminating the threats themselves although the study and prediction of the threats is an imminent part of the field. The basic level of emergency management are the various kinds of search and rescue activity.
Federal Emergency Management Agency	The Federal Emergency Management Agency is an agency of the United States Department of Homeland Security, initially created by Presidential Reorganization Plan No. 3 of 1978 and implemented by two Executive Orders. On 1 April 1979. The primary purpose of federal\ emergency\ management\ agency is to coordinate the response to a disaster that has occurred in the United States and that overwhelms the resources of local and state authorities. The governor of the state in which the disaster occurs must declare a state of emergency and formally request from the president that federal\ emergency\ management\ agency and the federal government respond to the disaster.
Witness protection	Witness protection is protection of a threatened witness or any person involved in the justice system, including defendants and other clients, before, during and after a trial, usually by police. While a witness may only require protection until the conclusion of a trial, some witnesses are provided with a new identity and may live out the rest of their lives under government protection.

Witness protection is usually required in trials against organized crime, where law enforcement sees a risk for witnesses to be intimidated by colleagues of defendants. |
| Ponzi scheme | A Ponzi scheme is a fraudulent investment operation that pays returns to its investors from their own money or the money paid by subsequent investors, rather than from profit earned by the individual or organization running the operation. The Ponzi scheme usually entices new investors by offering higher returns than other investments, in the form of short-term returns that are either abnormally high or unusually consistent. Perpetuation of the high returns requires an ever-increasing flow of money from new investors to keep the scheme going. |

1. What Is Criminal Justice?

Sarbanes-Oxley Act	The Sarbanes-Oxley Act of 2002, also known as the 'Public Company Accounting Reform and Investor Protection Act' (in the Senate) and 'Corporate and Auditing Accountability and Responsibility Act' (in the House) and more commonly called Sarbanes-Oxley, Sarbox or SOX, is a United States federal law that set new or enhanced standards for all U.S. public company boards, management and public accounting firms. S. Senator Paul Sarbanes (D-MD) and U.S. Representative Michael G. Oxley (R-OH). As a result of SOX, top management must now individually certify the accuracy of financial information.
Corporate crime	In criminology, corporate crime refers to crimes committed either by a corporation (i.e., a business entity having a separate legal personality from the natural persons that manage its activities), or by individuals acting on behalf of a corporation or other business entity . Some negative behaviours by corporations may not actually be criminal; laws vary between jurisdictions. For example, some jurisdictions allow insider trading.
White-collar crime	White-collar crime is a financially motivated, economic, non-violent crime committed for illegal monetary gain. Within the field of criminology, white-collar crime initially was defined by Edwin Sutherland in 1939 as 'a crime committed by a person of respectability and high social status in the course of his occupation' (1939). Sutherland was a proponent of Symbolic Interactionism, and believed that criminal behavior was learned from interpersonal interaction with others.
Sex Offender	A sex offender is a person who has committed a sex crime or in some instances even mere public urination. What constitutes a sex crime differs by culture and legal jurisdiction. Most jurisdictions compile their laws into sections, such as traffic, assault and sexual.
Community policing	Community policing is a policing strategy and philosophy based on the notion that community interaction and support can help control crime and reduce fear, with community members helping to identify suspects, detain offenders, bring problems to the attention of police, or otherwise target the social problems which give rise to a crime problem in Community policing is a philosophy that promotes organizational strategies that support the systematic use of partnerships and problem-solving techniques, which proactively address the immediate conditions that give rise to public safety issues such as crime, social disorder, and fear of crime. Community Policing consists of three key components: Community Partnerships: Collaborative partnerships between the law enforcement agency and the individuals and organizations they serve to develop solutions to problems and increase trust in police. These partnerships are forged in conjunction with other government agencies,community members and groups, human and social service providers, private businesses, and the media.
Christopher Commission	The Independent Commission on the Los Angeles Police Department, informally known as the Christopher Commission, was formed in April 1991, in the wake of the Rodney King beating, by then-mayor of Los Angeles Tom Bradley.

	It was chaired by attorney Warren Christopher (who later became U.S. Secretary of State under President Bill Clinton). 'The commission was created to conduct 'a full and fair examination of the structure and operation of the LAPD,' including its recruitment and training practices, internal disciplinary system, and citizen complaint system.' However, with the election of Richard Riordan, these reforms were put on hold.
Social justice	Social justice is defined as justice exercised within a society, particularly as it is exercised by and among the various social classes of that society. A socially just society is defined by its advocates and practitioners as being based on the principles of equality and solidarity; this pedagogy also maintains that the socially just society both understands and values human rights, as well as recognizing the dignity of every human being. The Constitution of the International Labour Organization affirms that 'universal and lasting peace can be established only if it is based upon social justice.' Furthermore, the Vienna Declaration and Programme of Action treats social justice as a purpose of the human rights education.
Computer fraud	Computer fraud is the use of information technology to commit fraud. In the United States, computer fraud is specifically proscribed by the Computer Fraud and Abuse Act, which provides for jail time and fines. Notable incidentsUnauthorized access at North Bay Abdulswamad Nino Macapayad, a former accounts payable clerk for North Bay Health Care Group, admitted to using her computer to access North Bay's accounting software without authorization, and in turn issued various checks payable to herself and others.
CrimeStat	CrimeStat is a crime mapping software program. CrimeStat is Windows-based program that conducts spatial and statistical analysis and is designed to interface with a geographic information system (GIS). The program is developed by Ned Levine & Associates, with funding by the National Institute of Justice (NIJ), an agency of the United States Department of Justice.
Fraud	In criminal law, a fraud is an intentional deception made for personal gain or to damage another individual; the related adjective is fraudulent. The specific legal definition varies by legal jurisdiction. Fraud is a crime, and also a civil law violation.
Domestic violence	Domestic violence, spousal abuse, battering, family violence, and intimate partner violence (IPV), is defined as a pattern of abusive behaviors by one partner against another in an intimate relationship such as marriage, dating, family, or cohabitation. Domestic violence, so defined, has many forms, including physical aggression or assault (hitting, kicking, biting, shoving, restraining, slapping, throwing objects), or threats thereof; sexual abuse; emotional abuse; controlling or domineering; intimidation; stalking; passive/covert abuse (e.g., neglect); and economic deprivation.

1. What Is Criminal Justice?

Crime control	Crime control refers to methods taken to reduce crime in a society. Penology often focuses on the use of criminal penalties as a means of deterring people from committing crimes and temporarily or permanently incapacitating those who have already committed crimes from re-offending. Crime prevention is also widely implemented in some countries, through government police and, in many cases, private policing methods such as private security and home defense.
Due process	Due process is the legal requirement that the state must respect all of the legal rights that are owed to a person. Due process balances the power of law of the land and protects the individual person from it. When a government harms a person without following the exact course of the law, this constitutes a due-process violation, which offends against the rule of law.
Social control	Social control refers generally to societal and political mechanisms or processes that regulate individual and group behavior in an attempt to gain conformity and compliance to the rules of a given society, state, or social group. Sociologists identify two basic forms of social control:•Informal means of control - Internalisation of norms and values by a process known as socialization, which is defined as 'the process by which an individual, born with behavioral potentialities of enormously wide range, is led to develop actual behavior which is confined to the narrower range of what is acceptable for him by the group standards.'•Formal means of social control - External sanctions enforced by government to prevent the establishment of chaos or anomie in society. Some theorists, such as Émile Durkheim, refer to this form of control as regulation While the concept of social control has been around since the formation of organized sociology, the meaning has been altered over time.
Criminology	Criminology is the scientific study of the nature, extent, causes, and control of criminal behavior in both the individual and in society. Criminology is an interdisciplinary field in the behavioral sciences, drawing especially upon the research of sociologists (particularly in the sociology of deviance), psychologists and psychiatrists, social anthropologists as well as on writings in law. Areas of research in criminology include the incidence, forms, causes and consequences of crime, as well as social and governmental regulations and reaction to crime.
CAN-SPAM Act	The CAN-SPAM Act of 2003 (15 U.S.C. 7701, et seq., Public Law No. 108-187, was S.877 of the 108th United States Congress), signed into law by President George W. Bush on December 16, 2003, establishes the United States' first national standards for the sending of commercial e-mail and requires the Federal Trade Commission (FTC) to enforce its provisions. The acronym CAN-SPAM derives from the bill's full name: Controlling the Assault of Non-Solicited Pornography And Marketing Act of 2003. This is also a play on the usual term for unsolicited email of this type, spam. The bill was sponsored in Congress by Senators Conrad Burns and Ron Wyden.

Probation	Probation developed from the efforts of a philanthropist, John Augustus, who looked for ways to rehabilitate the behavior of criminals. Probation literally means testing of strange behaviour or abilities. In a legal sense, an offender on probation is ordered to follow certain conditions set forth by the court, often under the supervision of a probation officer.
Multiculturalism	Multiculturalism relates to communities containing multiple cultures. The term is used in two broad ways, either descriptively or normatively. As a descriptive term, it usually refers to the simple fact of cultural diversity: it is generally applied to the demographic make-up of a specific place, sometime at the organizational level, e.g. schools, businesses, neighbourhoods, cities, or nations.

CHAPTER QUIZ: KEY TERMS, PEOPLE, PLACES, CONCEPTS

1. The _____ of 2002, also known as the 'Public Company Accounting Reform and Investor Protection Act' (in the Senate) and 'Corporate and Auditing Accountability and Responsibility Act' (in the House) and more commonly called Sarbanes-Oxley, Sarbox or SOX, is a United States federal law that set new or enhanced standards for all U.S. public company boards, management and public accounting firms. S. Senator Paul Sarbanes (D-MD) and U.S. Representative Michael G. Oxley (R-OH). As a result of SOX, top management must now individually certify the accuracy of financial information.

    a. Second Chance Act
    b. Securities Exchange Act of 1934
    c. Sarbanes-Oxley Act
    d. Speedy Trial Act

2. _____ is the system of practices and institutions of governments directed at upholding social control, deterring and mitigating crime, or sanctioning those who violate laws with criminal penalties and rehabilitation efforts. Those accused of crime have protections against abuse of investigatory and prosecution powers. Goals

    In the United States, _____ policy has been guided by the 1967 President's Commission on Law Enforcement and Administration of Justice, which issued a ground-breaking report 'The Challenge of Crime in a Free Society'.

    a. National Criminal Justice Reference Service
    b. Homeland Security Act
    c. Fair and Accurate Credit Transactions Act
    d. Criminal justice

3. . _____ refers to methods taken to reduce crime in a society. Penology often focuses on the use of criminal penalties as a means of deterring people from committing crimes and temporarily or permanently incapacitating those who have already committed crimes from re-offending.

Crime prevention is also widely implemented in some countries, through government police and, in many cases, private policing methods such as private security and home defense.

a. Prison rape
b. Larceny
c. pickpocketing
d. Crime control

4. _____ is the use of information technology to commit fraud. In the United States, _____ is specifically proscribed by the _____ and Abuse Act, which provides for jail time and fines. Notable incidentsUnauthorized access at North Bay

Abdulswamad Nino Macapayad, a former accounts payable clerk for North Bay Health Care Group, admitted to using her computer to access North Bay's accounting software without authorization, and in turn issued various checks payable to herself and others.

a. Computer fraud
b. Wickersham Commission
c. National Commission on Law Observance and Enforcement
d. Fair and Accurate Credit Transactions Act

5. _____, spousal abuse, battering, family violence, and intimate partner violence (IPV), is defined as a pattern of abusive behaviors by one partner against another in an intimate relationship such as marriage, dating, family, or cohabitation. _____, so defined, has many forms, including physical aggression or assault (hitting, kicking, biting, shoving, restraining, slapping, throwing objects), or threats thereof; sexual abuse; emotional abuse; controlling or domineering; intimidation; stalking; passive/covert abuse (e.g., neglect); and economic deprivation.

Alcohol consumption and mental illness can be co-morbid with abuse, and present additional challenges in eliminating _____.

a. Homeland Security Act
b. Larceny
c. pickpocketing
d. Domestic violence

ANSWER KEY
1. What Is Criminal Justice?

1. c
2. d
3. d
4. a
5. d

You can take the complete Chapter Practice Test

for 1. What Is Criminal Justice?
on all key terms, persons, places, and concepts.

Online 99 Cents

http://www.epub4670.4.23017.1.cram101.com/

Use www.Cram101.com for all your study needs

including Cram101's online interactive problem solving labs in

chemistry, statistics, mathematics, and more.

2. The Crime Picture

CHAPTER OUTLINE: KEY TERMS, PEOPLE, PLACES, CONCEPTS

	Identity theft
	Crime statistics
	Criminal justice
	National Incident-Based Reporting System
	Hate crime
	Violence Against Women Act
	Crime control
	Law enforcement
	Violent crime
	Clearance rate
	Property crime
	David Berkowitz
	Ted Kaczynski
	Unborn Victims of Violence Act
	Mass murder
	Community policing
	Deadly force
	Ponzi scheme
	Date rape
	Date rape drug
	Sex Offender

Aryan Brotherhood

Knapp Commission

Aggravation

Texas Syndicate

Burglary

Forcible entry

Ruby Ridge

Larceny

National Association for the Advancement of Colored People

Domestic violence

Durham rule

Insanity defense

Intellectual Property

CAN-SPAM Act

Mortgage fraud

Carjacking

Motor vehicle theft

Appellate court

Dark figure of crime

Witness protection

Victimless crime

CHAPTER OUTLINE: KEY TERMS, PEOPLE, PLACES, CONCEPTS

_____ | Speedy trial

_____ | Stalking

_____ | Cyberstalking

_____ | Corporate crime

_____ | Fraud

_____ | White-collar crime

_____ | Cosa Nostra

_____ | National White Collar Crime Center

_____ | Sarbanes-Oxley Act

_____ | Organized crime

_____ | Transnational organized crime

_____ | Brady Handgun Violence Prevention Act

_____ | Computer crime

_____ | CompStat

_____ | Computer fraud

_____ | Computer Virus

_____ | Malware

_____ | Computer security

_____ | Terrorism

_____ | Phishing

_____ | Department of Homeland Security

2. The Crime Picture

	Cyberterrorism
	International crime

Identity theft	Identity theft is a form of fraud or cheating of another person's identity in which someone pretends to be someone else by assuming that person's identity, typically in order to access resources or obtain credit and other benefits in that person's name. The victim of identity theft can suffer adverse consequences if he or she is held accountable for the perpetrator's actions. Organizations and individuals who are duped or defrauded by the identity thief can also suffer adverse consequences and losses, and to that extent are also victims.
Crime statistics	Crime statistics attempt to provide statistical measures of the crime in societies. Given that crime is usually secretive by nature, measurements of it are likely to be inaccurate. Several methods for measuring crime exist, including household surveys, hospital or insurance records, and compilations by police and similar law enforcement agencies.
Criminal justice	Criminal justice is the system of practices and institutions of governments directed at upholding social control, deterring and mitigating crime, or sanctioning those who violate laws with criminal penalties and rehabilitation efforts. Those accused of crime have protections against abuse of investigatory and prosecution powers. Goals In the United States, criminal justice policy has been guided by the 1967 President's Commission on Law Enforcement and Administration of Justice, which issued a ground-breaking report 'The Challenge of Crime in a Free Society'.
National Incident-Based Reporting System	National Incident-Based Reporting System is an incident-based reporting system used by law enforcement agencies in the United States for collecting and reporting data on crimes. Local, state and federal agencies generate National Incident Based Reporting System data from their records management systems. Data is collected on every incident and arrest in the Group A offense category.
Hate crime	In both crime and law, hate crimes (also known as bias-motivated crimes, or a race hate) occur when a perpetrator targets a victim because of his or her perceived membership in a certain social group.

Examples of such groups include but are not limited to: racial group, religion, sexual orientation, ethnicity, or gender identity.

A hate crime is a category used to describe bias-motivated violence: 'assault, injury, and murder on the basis of certain personal characteristics: different appearance, different color, different nationality, different language, different religion.'

'Hate crime' generally refers to criminal acts that are seen to have been motivated by bias against one or more of the types above, or of their derivatives.

Violence Against Women Act	The Violence Against Women Act of 1994 is a United States federal law (Title IV, sec. 40001-40703 of the Violent Crime Control and Law Enforcement Act of 1994, H.R. 3355) signed as Pub.L. 103-322 by President Bill Clinton on September 13, 1994. The Act provides $1.6 billion toward investigation and prosecution of violent crimes against women, imposes automatic and mandatory restitution on those convicted, and allows civil redress in cases prosecutors chose to leave unprosecuted. The Act also establishes the Office on Violence Against Women within the Department of Justice. Male victims of domestic violence, dating violence, sexual assault, and stalking may also be covered.
Crime control	Crime control refers to methods taken to reduce crime in a society. Penology often focuses on the use of criminal penalties as a means of deterring people from committing crimes and temporarily or permanently incapacitating those who have already committed crimes from re-offending. Crime prevention is also widely implemented in some countries, through government police and, in many cases, private policing methods such as private security and home defense.
Law enforcement	Law enforcement broadly refers to any system by which some members of society act in an organized manner to promote adherence to the law by discovering and punishing persons who violate the rules and norms governing that society. Although the term may encompass entities such as courts and prisons, it is most frequently applied to those who directly engage in patrols or surveillance to dissuade and discover criminal activity, and those who investigate crimes and apprehend offenders. Furthermore, although law enforcement may be most concerned with the prevention and punishment of crimes, organizations exist to discourage a wide variety of non-criminal violations of rules and norms, effected through the imposition of less severe consequences.
Violent crime	A violent crime is a crime in which the offender uses or threatens to use violent force upon the victim. This entails both crimes in which the violent act is the objective, such as murder, as well as crimes in which violence is the means to an end, (including criminal ends) such as robbery. Violent crimes include crimes committed with weapons.
Clearance rate	In criminal justice, clearance rate is calculated by dividing the number of crimes that are 'cleared' (a charge being laid) by the total number of crimes recorded.

2. The Crime Picture

Clearance rates are used by various groups as a measure of crimes solved by the police.

Clearance rates can be problematic for measuring the performance of police services and for comparing various police services.

Property crime	Property crime is a category of crime that includes, among other crimes, burglary, larceny, theft, motor vehicle theft, arson, shoplifting, and vandalism. Property crime only involves the taking of money or property, and does not involve force or threat of force against a victim. Although robbery involves taking property, it is classified as a violent crime, as force or threat of force on an individual that is present is involved in contrast to burglary which is typically of an unoccupied dwelling or other unoccupied building.
David Berkowitz	David Berkowitz, also known as the Son of Sam and the .44 Caliber Killer, is an American serial killer convicted of a series of shooting attacks that began in the summer of 1976. Perpetrated with a .44 caliber Bulldog revolver, the shootings continued for over a year, leaving six victims dead and seven others wounded. As the toll mounted, David Berkowitz eluded a massive police manhunt while leaving brazen letters which promised more and more murders. Highly publicized in the press, the killings terrorized the people of New York City and achieved worldwide notoriety.
Ted Kaczynski	Ted Kaczynski, also known as the 'Unabomber', is an American terrorist, mathematician, social critic, anarchist, and Neo-Luddite. Between 1978 and 1995, Kaczynski engaged in a nation-wide bombing campaign against modern technology, planting or mailing numerous home-made bombs, killing three people and injuring 23 others. Kaczynski was born in Chicago, Illinois, where, as a child prodigy, he excelled academically from an early age.
Unborn Victims of Violence Act	The Unborn Victims of Violence Act of 2004 (Public Law 108-212) is a United States law which recognizes a child in utero as a legal victim, if he or she is injured or killed during the commission of any of over 60 listed federal crimes of violence. The law defines 'child in utero' as 'a member of the species Homo sapiens, at any stage of development, who is carried in the womb'. The law is codified in two sections of the United States Code: Title 18, Chapter 1 (Crimes), §1841 (18 USC 1841) and Title 10, Chapter 22 (Uniform Code of Military Justice) §919a (Article 119a).
Mass murder	Mass murder is the act of murdering a large number of people, typically at the same time or over a relatively short period of time. According to the FBI, mass murder is defined as four or more murders occurring during a particular event with no cooling-off period between the murders. A mass murder typically occurs in a single location in which a number of victims are killed by an individual or more.

Community policing	Community policing is a policing strategy and philosophy based on the notion that community interaction and support can help control crime and reduce fear, with community members helping to identify suspects, detain offenders, bring problems to the attention of police, or otherwise target the social problems which give rise to a crime problem in Community policing is a philosophy that promotes organizational strategies that support the systematic use of partnerships and problem-solving techniques, which proactively address the immediate conditions that give rise to public safety issues such as crime, social disorder, and fear of crime. Community Policing consists of three key components: Community Partnerships: Collaborative partnerships between the law enforcement agency and the individuals and organizations they serve to develop solutions to problems and increase trust in police. These partnerships are forged in conjunction with other government agencies,community members and groups, human and social service providers, private businesses, and the media.
Deadly force	Deadly force, as defined by the United States Armed Forces, is the force which a person uses, causing-or that a person knows, or should know, would create a substantial risk of causing-death or serious bodily harm. In most jurisdictions, the use of deadly force is justified only under conditions of extreme necessity as a last resort, when all lesser means have failed or cannot reasonably be employed. Firearms, bladed weapons, explosives, and vehicles are among those weapons the use of which is considered deadly force.
Ponzi scheme	A Ponzi scheme is a fraudulent investment operation that pays returns to its investors from their own money or the money paid by subsequent investors, rather than from profit earned by the individual or organization running the operation. The Ponzi scheme usually entices new investors by offering higher returns than other investments, in the form of short-term returns that are either abnormally high or unusually consistent. Perpetuation of the high returns requires an ever-increasing flow of money from new investors to keep the scheme going.
Date rape	The term date rape is widely used but can be misleading. The perpetrator of the crime might not be dating the victim; it could be a friend, acquaintance or stranger. Commonly, date rape is referring to drug-facilitated sexual assault and/or acquaintance rape.
Date rape drug	A date rape drug, is any drug that can be used to assist in the execution of drug facilitated sexual assault (DFSA). The most common types of DFSA are those in which a victim ingested drugs willingly for recreational purposes, or had them administered surreptitiously: it is the latter type of assault that the term 'date rape drug' most often refers to.

2. The Crime Picture

Sex Offender	A sex offender is a person who has committed a sex crime or in some instances even mere public urination. What constitutes a sex crime differs by culture and legal jurisdiction. Most jurisdictions compile their laws into sections, such as traffic, assault and sexual.
Aryan Brotherhood	The Aryan Brotherhood, the AB, Alice Baker, or the One-Two, is a white supremacist prison gang and organized crime syndicate in the United States with about 20,000 members in and out of prison. According to the Federal Bureau of Investigation (FBI), the gang makes up less than 1% of the prison population, but it is responsible for up to 20% of murders in the federal prison system. The AB has focused on the economic activities typical of organized crime entities, particularly drug trafficking, extortion, inmate prostitution, and murder-for-hire.
Knapp Commission	The Knapp Commission stemmed from a five-member panel initially formed in April 1970 by Mayor John V. Lindsay to investigate corruption within the New York City Police Department. The creation of the commission was largely a result of the publicity generated by the public revelations of police corruption made by Patrolman Frank Serpico and Sergeant David Durk. Investigation and public hearings

While the Knapp Commission began its investigation of corruption in the police department in June 1970, public hearings didn't start until October 18, 1971. In addition to the testimony of lamplighters Serpico and Durk, testimony from dozens of other witnesses, including former Police Commissioner Howard R. Leary, corrupt patrolmen and the victims of police shakedowns, were heard. |
| Aggravation | Aggravation, in law, is 'any circumstance attending the commission of a crime or tort which increases its guilt or enormity or adds to its injurious consequences, but which is above and beyond the essential constituents of the crime or tort itself.'

Aggravated assault, for example, is usually differentiated from simple assault by the offender's intent (e.g., to murder or to rape), the extent of injury to the victim, or the use of a deadly weapon. An aggravating circumstance is a kind of attendant circumstance and the opposite of an extenuating or mitigating circumstance, which decreases guilt. |
| Texas Syndicate | The Texas Syndicate is a mostly Texas-based prison gang that includes Hispanic and at one time, White (non-Hispanic) members. The Texas Syndicate, unlike La Eme or Nuestra Familia, has been more associated or allied with Mexican immigrant prisoners, known as 'border brothers', while La Eme and the NF tend to be more composed of US-born/raised Hispanics.

It was established in the 1970s at Folsom Prison in California in direct response to the other California prison gangs (notably the Aryan Brotherhood and Mexican Mafia), which were attempting to prey on native Texas inmates. |

Burglary	Burglary is a crime, the essence of which is illegal entry into a building for the purposes of committing an offence. Usually that offence will be theft, but most jurisdictions specify others which fall within the ambit of burglary. To engage in the act of burglary is to burgle or to burglarize .
Forcible entry	Forcible entry is defined by Merriam-Webster's Dictionary of Law as the unlawful taking of possession of real property by force or threats of force or unlawful entry into or onto another's property, especially when accompanied by force.
	The term is also sometimes used for entry by military, police, or emergency personnel. For the fire service, forcible entry is defined by the International Fire Service Training Association (IFSTA) as:
	and when accessing doorways can be defined as 'through the lock' or 'around the lock' depending on the techniques used.
Ruby Ridge	Ruby Ridge was the site of a deadly confrontation and siege in northern Idaho in 1992 between Randy Weaver, his family, Weaver's friend Kevin Harris, and agents of the United States Marshals Service and Federal Bureau of Investigation. It resulted in the death of Weaver's son Sammy, his wife Vicki, and Deputy US Marshal William Francis Degan.
	At the subsequent federal criminal trial of Weaver and Harris, Weaver's attorney Gerry Spence made accusations of 'criminal wrongdoing' against every agency involved in the incident: the FBI, USMS, the Bureau of Alcohol, Tobacco, Firearms and Explosives (ATF), and the United States Attorney's Office (USAO) for Idaho.
Larceny	Larceny is a crime involving the wrongful acquisition of the personal property of another person. It was an offense under the common law of England and became an offense in jurisdictions which incorporated the common law of England into their own law. It has been abolished in England and Wales, Northern Ireland and the Republic of Ireland.
National Association for the Advancement of Colored People	The National Association for the Advancement of Colored People is an African-American civil rights organization in the United States, formed in 1909. Its mission is 'to ensure the political, educational, social, and economic equality of rights of all persons and to eliminate racial hatred and racial discrimination'. Its name, retained in accordance with tradition, uses the once common term colored people.
	The NAACP bestows the annual Image Awards for achievement in the arts and entertainment, and the annual Spingarn Medals for outstanding positive achievement of any kind, on deserving black Americans.
Domestic violence	Domestic violence, spousal abuse, battering, family violence, and intimate partner violence (IPV), is defined as a pattern of abusive behaviors by one partner against another in an intimate relationship such as marriage, dating, family, or cohabitation.

2. The Crime Picture

Domestic violence, so defined, has many forms, including physical aggression or assault (hitting, kicking, biting, shoving, restraining, slapping, throwing objects), or threats thereof; sexual abuse; emotional abuse; controlling or domineering; intimidation; stalking; passive/covert abuse (e.g., neglect); and economic deprivation.

Alcohol consumption and mental illness can be co-morbid with abuse, and present additional challenges in eliminating domestic violence.

Durham rule

The Durham Rule or 'product test' was adopted by the United States Court of Appeals for the District of Columbia Circuit in 1954, in the case of Durham v. U.S. (214 F.2d 862), and states that '... an accused is not criminally responsible if his unlawful act was the product of mental disease or defect'. Durham was later overturned in the case U.S. v. Brawner, 471 F.2d 969 (1972). After the 1970s, U.S. jurisdictions have tended to not recognize this argument as it places emphasis on 'mental disease or defect' and thus on testimony by psychiatrists and is argued to be somewhat ambiguous.

Insanity defense

In criminal trials, the insanity defense is where the defendant claims that he or she was not responsible for his or her actions due to mental health problems (psychiatric illness or mental handicap). The exemption of the insane from full criminal punishment dates back to at least the Code of Hammurabi. There are different definitions of legal insanity, such as the M'Naghten Rules, the Durham Rule, the American Legal Institute definition, and various miscellaneous provisions .

Intellectual Property

Intellectual property is a legal concept which refers to creations of the mind for which exclusive rights are recognized. Under intellectual property law, owners are granted certain exclusive rights to a variety of intangible assets, such as musical, literary, and artistic works; discoveries and inventions; and words, phrases, symbols, and designs. Common types of intellectual property rights include copyright, trademarks, patents, industrial design rights, trade dress, and in some jurisdictions trade secrets.

CAN-SPAM Act

The CAN-SPAM Act of 2003 (15 U.S.C. 7701, et seq., Public Law No. 108-187, was S.877 of the 108th United States Congress), signed into law by President George W. Bush on December 16, 2003, establishes the United States' first national standards for the sending of commercial e-mail and requires the Federal Trade Commission (FTC) to enforce its provisions.

The acronym CAN-SPAM derives from the bill's full name: Controlling the Assault of Non-Solicited Pornography And Marketing Act of 2003. This is also a play on the usual term for unsolicited email of this type, spam. The bill was sponsored in Congress by Senators Conrad Burns and Ron Wyden.

Mortgage fraud

Mortgage fraud is a crime in which the intent is to materially misrepresent or omit information on a mortgage loan application to obtain a loan or to obtain a larger loan than would have been obtained had the lender or borrower known the truth.

	In United States federal courts, mortgage fraud is prosecuted as wire fraud, bank fraud, mail fraud and money laundering, with penalties of up to thirty years imprisonment. As the incidence of mortgage fraud has risen over the past few years, states have also begun to enact their own penalties for mortgage fraud.
Carjacking	Carjacking is the unlawful seizure of automobile. It's also armed assault when the vehicle is occupied. Historically, such as in the rash of semi-trailer truck hijackings during the 1960s, the general term hijacking was used for that type of vehicle abduction, which did not often include kidnapping of the driver, and concentrated on the theft of the load, rather than the vehicle itself.
Motor vehicle theft	Motor vehicle theft is the criminal act of stealing or attempting to steal a motor vehicle (such as an automobile, truck, bus, coach, motorcycle, snowmobile, trailer). Nationwide in the US in 2005, there were an estimated 1.2 million motor vehicle thefts, or approximately 416.7 motor vehicles stolen for every 100,000 inhabitants. Property losses due to motor vehicle theft in 2005 were estimated at $7.6 billion.
Appellate court	An appellate court, commonly called an appeals court or court of appeals or appeal court, is any court of law that is empowered to hear an appeal of a trial court or other lower tribunal. In most jurisdictions, the court system is divided into at least three levels: the trial court, which initially hears cases and reviews evidence and testimony to determine the facts of the case; at least one intermediate appellate court; and a supreme court which primarily reviews the decisions of the intermediate courts. A jurisdiction's supreme court is that jurisdiction's highest appellate court.
Dark figure of crime	The dark figure of (or for) crime is a term employed by criminologists and sociologists to describe the amount of unreported or undiscovered crime, which calls into question the reliability of official crime statistics. Victim studies, such as the research associated with the British Crime Survey (BCS), are recent attempts to provide an insight into the amount of unreported crime. Unrecorded and unreported crime Not all the crimes that take place are reported to, or recorded by, the police. Given this, sociologists refer to the gap between the official level of crime and the amount of crime in the community as the dark figure of crime.
Witness protection	Witness protection is protection of a threatened witness or any person involved in the justice system, including defendants and other clients, before, during and after a trial, usually by police. While a witness may only require protection until the conclusion of a trial, some witnesses are provided with a new identity and may live out the rest of their lives under government protection.

2. The Crime Picture

Victimless crime	A victimless crime is a term used to refer to actions that have been ruled illegal but do not directly violate or threaten the rights of another individual. It often involves consensual acts in which two or more persons agree to commit a criminal offence in which no other person is involved. For example, in the United States current victimless crimes include prostitution, gambling, and illicit drug use.
Speedy trial	The Speedy Trial Clause of the Sixth Amendment to the United States Constitution provides that '[i]n all criminal prosecutions, the accused shall enjoy the right to a speedy . . . trial . . . .' The Clause protects the defendant from delay between the presentation of the indictment or similar charging instrument and the beginning of trial.
Stalking	Stalking is a term commonly used to refer to unwanted, obsessive attention by individuals (and sometimes groups of people) to others. Stalking behaviors are related to harassment and intimidation. The word 'stalking' is used, with some differing meanings, in psychology and psychiatry and also in some legal jurisdictions as a term for a criminal offense.
Cyberstalking	Cyberstalking is the use of the Internet or other electronic means to stalk or harass an individual, a group of individuals, or an organization. It may include the making of false accusations or statements of fact (as in defamation), monitoring, making threats, identity theft, damage to data or equipment, the solicitation of minors for sex, or gathering information that may be used to harass. The definition of 'harassment' must meet the criterion that a reasonable person, in possession of the same information, would regard it as sufficient to cause another reasonable person distress.
Corporate crime	In criminology, corporate crime refers to crimes committed either by a corporation (i.e., a business entity having a separate legal personality from the natural persons that manage its activities), or by individuals acting on behalf of a corporation or other business entity . Some negative behaviours by corporations may not actually be criminal; laws vary between jurisdictions. For example, some jurisdictions allow insider trading.
Fraud	In criminal law, a fraud is an intentional deception made for personal gain or to damage another individual; the related adjective is fraudulent. The specific legal definition varies by legal jurisdiction. Fraud is a crime, and also a civil law violation.
White-collar crime	White-collar crime is a financially motivated, economic, non-violent crime committed for illegal monetary gain. Within the field of criminology, white-collar crime initially was defined by Edwin Sutherland in 1939 as 'a crime committed by a person of respectability and high social status in the course of his occupation' (1939). Sutherland was a proponent of Symbolic Interactionism, and believed that criminal behavior was learned from interpersonal interaction with others.
Cosa Nostra	The Mafia (also known as Cosa Nostra, in English 'Our Thing') is a criminal syndicate that emerged in the mid-nineteenth century in Sicily, Italy.

	It is a loose association of criminal groups that share a common organizational structure and code of conduct, and whose common enterprise is protection racketeering. Each group, known as a 'family', 'clan', or 'cosca', claims sovereignty over a territory in which it operates its rackets - usually a town or village or a neighbourhood (borgata) of a larger city.
National White Collar Crime Center	The National White Collar Crime Center is a congressionally funded non-profit corporation that trains state and local law enforcement agencies in how to combat emerging economic and cyber crime problems. NW3C provides information and research to the general public in the prevention of economic and cyber crime. In their partnership with the Internet Crime Complaint Center, NW3C assists Internet crime victims by relaying their reports to the appropriate authorities at local, state, and federal levels.
Sarbanes-Oxley Act	The Sarbanes-Oxley Act of 2002, also known as the 'Public Company Accounting Reform and Investor Protection Act' (in the Senate) and 'Corporate and Auditing Accountability and Responsibility Act' (in the House) and more commonly called Sarbanes-Oxley, Sarbox or SOX, is a United States federal law that set new or enhanced standards for all U.S. public company boards, management and public accounting firms. S. Senator Paul Sarbanes (D-MD) and U.S. Representative Michael G. Oxley (R-OH). As a result of SOX, top management must now individually certify the accuracy of financial information.
Organized crime	Organized crime or criminal organizations are transnational, national, or local groupings of highly centralized enterprises run by criminals for the purpose of engaging in illegal activity, most commonly for monetary profit. Some criminal organizations, such as terrorist organizations, are politically motivated. Sometimes criminal organizations force people to do business with them, as when a gang extorts money from shopkeepers for so-called 'protection'.
Transnational organized crime	Transnational organized crime is organized crime coordinated across national borders, involving groups or networks of individuals working in more than one country to plan and execute illegal business ventures. In order to achieve their goals, these criminal groups utilize systematic violence and corruption. The most commonly seen transnational organized crimes are money laundering; human smuggling; cyber crime; and trafficking of humans, drugs, weapons, endangered species, body parts, or nuclear material.
Brady Handgun Violence Prevention Act	The Brady Handgun Violence Prevention Act is an Act of the United States Congress that instituted federal background checks on firearm purchasers in the United States. It was signed into law by President Bill Clinton on November 30, 1993, and went into effect on February 28, 1994. during an attempted assassination of President Ronald Reagan on March 30, 1981. Provisions

2. The Crime Picture

Computer crime	Computer crime refers to any crime that involves a computer and a network. The computer may have been used in the commission of a crime, or it may be the target. Netcrime refers to criminal exploitation of the Internet.
CompStat	CompStat--or COMPSTAT--(short for COMPuter STATistics or COMParative STATistics) is the name given to the New York City Police Department's accountability process and has since been replicated in many other departments. CompStat is a management philosophy or organizational management tool for police departments, roughly equivalent to Six Sigma or TQM, and is not a computer system or software package.
	Instead, CompStat is a multilayered dynamic approach to crime reduction, quality of life improvement, and personnel and resource management.
Computer fraud	Computer fraud is the use of information technology to commit fraud. In the United States, computer fraud is specifically proscribed by the Computer Fraud and Abuse Act, which provides for jail time and fines. Notable incidentsUnauthorized access at North Bay
	Abdulswamad Nino Macapayad, a former accounts payable clerk for North Bay Health Care Group, admitted to using her computer to access North Bay's accounting software without authorization, and in turn issued various checks payable to herself and others.
Computer Virus	A computer virus is a computer program that can replicate itself and spread from one computer to another. The term 'virus' is also commonly, but erroneously, used to refer to other types of malware, including but not limited to adware and spyware programs that do not have a reproductive ability.
	Malware includes computer viruses, computer worms, ransomware, trojan horses, keyloggers, most rootkits, spyware, dishonest adware, malicious BHOs and other malicious software.
Malware	Malware is software used or created by attackers to disrupt computer operation, gather sensitive information, or gain access to private computer systems. It can appear in the form of code, scripts, active content, and other software. 'Malware' is a general term used to refer to a variety of forms of hostile or intrusive software.
Computer security	Computer security is a branch of computer technology known as information security as applied to computers and networks. The objective of computer security includes protection of information and property from theft, corruption, or natural disaster, while allowing the information and property to remain accessible and productive to its intended users. The term computer system security means the collective processes and mechanisms by which sensitive and valuable information and services are protected from publication, tampering or collapse by unauthorized activities or untrustworthy individuals and unplanned events respectively.

2. The Crime Picture

Terrorism	Terrorism is the systematic use of terror, often violent, especially as a means of coercion. In the international community, however, terrorism has no legally binding, criminal law definition. Common definitions of terrorism refer only to those violent acts which are intended to create fear (terror), are perpetrated for a religious, political or, ideological goal; and deliberately target or disregard the safety of non-combatants (civilians).
Phishing	Phishing is the act of attempting to acquire information such as usernames, passwords, and credit card details (and sometimes, indirectly, money) by masquerading as a trustworthy entity in an electronic communication. Communications purporting to be from popular social web sites, auction sites, online payment processors or IT administrators are commonly used to lure the unsuspecting public. Phishing emails may contain links to websites that are infected with malware.
Department of Homeland Security	The Department of Homeland Security is a cabinet department of the United States federal government, created in response to the September 11 attacks, and with the primary responsibilities of protecting the United States of America and U.S. territories (including protectorates) from and responding to terrorist attacks, man-made accidents, and natural disasters. The Department of Homeland Security, and not the United States Department of the Interior, is equivalent to the Interior ministries of other countries. In fiscal year 2011, DHS was allocated a budget of $98.8 billion and spent, net, $66.4 billion.
Cyberterrorism	Cyberterrorism is the use of Internet based attacks in terrorist activities, including acts of deliberate, large-scale disruption of computer networks, especially of personal computers attached to the Internet, by the means of tools such as computer viruses. Cyberterrorism is a controversial term. Some authors choose a very narrow definition, relating to deployments, by known terrorist organizations, of disruption attacks against information systems for the primary purpose of creating alarm and panic.
International crime	International crime may refer to:•Crime against international law•Crime against humanity•Crime against peace•War crime•International criminal law or it may refer to transnational crimes. The four biggest areas of transnational crime are:•Drug trafficking•Arms trafficking•Money laundering•Smuggling of cultural artifacts Trans-national trafficking in human beings receives a great deal of attention by international bodies because of its particularly intimate nature. It may also refer to:•International Crime a film directed by Charles Lamont.

2. The Crime Picture

1. _____ is the systematic use of terror, often violent, especially as a means of coercion. In the international community, however, _____ has no legally binding, criminal law definition. Common definitions of _____ refer only to those violent acts which are intended to create fear (terror), are perpetrated for a religious, political or, ideological goal; and deliberately target or disregard the safety of non-combatants (civilians).

    a. Terrorism
    b. National Consortium for the Study of Terrorism and Responses to Terrorism
    c. Critical infrastructure
    d. Curfew

2. In both crime and law, _____s (also known as bias-motivated crimes, or a race hate) occur when a perpetrator targets a victim because of his or her perceived membership in a certain social group. Examples of such groups include but are not limited to: racial group, religion, sexual orientation, ethnicity, or gender identity.

    A _____ is a category used to describe bias-motivated violence: 'assault, injury, and murder on the basis of certain personal characteristics: different appearance, different color, different nationality, different language, different religion.'

    '_____' generally refers to criminal acts that are seen to have been motivated by bias against one or more of the types above, or of their derivatives.

    a. Homeland Security Act
    b. Hate crime
    c. Prison Rape Elimination Act
    d. DNA testing

3. _____ is the system of practices and institutions of governments directed at upholding social control, deterring and mitigating crime, or sanctioning those who violate laws with criminal penalties and rehabilitation efforts. Those accused of crime have protections against abuse of investigatory and prosecution powers. Goals

    In the United States, _____ policy has been guided by the 1967 President's Commission on Law Enforcement and Administration of Justice, which issued a ground-breaking report 'The Challenge of Crime in a Free Society'.

    a. National Criminal Justice Reference Service
    b. Homeland Security Act
    c. Criminal justice
    d. DNA testing

4. . _____ is the unlawful seizure of automobile. It's also armed assault when the vehicle is occupied. Historically, such as in the rash of semi-trailer truck hijackings during the 1960s, the general term hijacking was used for that type of vehicle abduction, which did not often include kidnapping of the driver, and concentrated on the theft of the load, rather than the vehicle itself.

    a. hijacking

b. Carjacking

c. Homeland Security Act

d. UCL Jill Dando Institute

5. _____ is a form of fraud or cheating of another person's identity in which someone pretends to be someone else by assuming that person's identity, typically in order to access resources or obtain credit and other benefits in that person's name. The victim of _____ can suffer adverse consequences if he or she is held accountable for the perpetrator's actions. Organizations and individuals who are duped or defrauded by the identity thief can also suffer adverse consequences and losses, and to that extent are also victims.

a. DNA profiling

b. photo identification

c. Genetic fingerprinting

d. Identity theft

1. a

2. b

3. c

4. b

5. d

You can take the complete Chapter Practice Test

for 2. The Crime Picture
on all key terms, persons, places, and concepts.

Online 99 Cents

http://www.epub4670.4.23017.2.cram101.com/

Use www.Cram101.com for all your study needs

including Cram101's online interactive problem solving labs in

chemistry, statistics, mathematics, and more.

3. Criminal Law

Criminal law

CAN-SPAM Act

Common law

Penal code

Statutory law

Law enforcement

Ruby Ridge

Law commission

CrimeStat

Procedural law

Christopher Commission

Administrative law

Ponzi scheme

Speedy trial

Witness protection

Espionage

Inchoate offense

Treason

Actus reus

Community policing

Computer fraud

CHAPTER OUTLINE: KEY TERMS, PEOPLE, PLACES, CONCEPTS

Fraud

Hate crime

Mortgage fraud

Criminal negligence

Mens rea

Strict liability

Principle of legality

Aryan Brotherhood

Mann Act

Corpus delicti

Malice aforethought

Manslaughter

Alibi

Deadly force

Right of self-defense

Self-defense

Probation

Domestic violence

Duress

Resisting unlawful arrest

Durham rule

	Innocence Protection Act
	Insanity defense
	Irresistible impulse
	Model Penal Code
	Jurisdiction
	Insanity Defense Reform Act
	Due process
	Double Jeopardy
	Entrapment
	Collateral estoppel
	Prosecutorial misconduct

CHAPTER HIGHLIGHTS & NOTES: KEY TERMS, PEOPLE, PLACES, CONCEPTS

Criminal law	Criminal law is the body of law that relates to crime. It regulates social conduct and proscribes threatening, harming, or otherwise endangering the health, safety, and moral welfare of people. It includes the punishment of people who violate these laws.
CAN-SPAM Act	The CAN-SPAM Act of 2003 (15 U.S.C. 7701, et seq., Public Law No. 108-187, was S.877 of the 108th United States Congress), signed into law by President George W. Bush on December 16, 2003, establishes the United States' first national standards for the sending of commercial e-mail and requires the Federal Trade Commission (FTC) to enforce its provisions.

The acronym CAN-SPAM derives from the bill's full name: Controlling the Assault of Non-Solicited Pornography And Marketing Act of 2003. This is also a play on the usual term for unsolicited email of this type, spam. |

Common law	Common law, is law developed by judges through decisions of courts and similar tribunals, as opposed to statutes adopted through the legislative process or regulations issued by the executive branch. A 'common law system' is a legal system that gives great precedential weight to common law, on the principle that it is unfair to treat similar facts differently on different occasions. The body of precedent is called 'common law' and it binds future decisions.
Penal code	A criminal code (or penal code) is a document which compiles all, or a significant amount of, a particular jurisdiction's criminal law. Typically a criminal code will contain offences which are recognised in the jurisdiction, penalties which might be imposed for these offences and some general provisions (such as definitions and prohibitions on retroactive prosecution). Criminal codes are relatively common in civil law jurisdictions, which tend to build legal systems around codes and principles which are relatively abstract and apply them on a case by case basis.
Statutory law	Statutory law is written law (as opposed to oral or customary law) set down by a legislature (as opposed to regulatory law promulgated by the executive or common law of the judiciary) or by a legislator (in the case of an absolute monarchy). Statutes may originate with national, state legislatures or local municipalities. Statutory laws are subordinate to the higher constitutional laws of the land.
Law enforcement	Law enforcement broadly refers to any system by which some members of society act in an organized manner to promote adherence to the law by discovering and punishing persons who violate the rules and norms governing that society. Although the term may encompass entities such as courts and prisons, it is most frequently applied to those who directly engage in patrols or surveillance to dissuade and discover criminal activity, and those who investigate crimes and apprehend offenders. Furthermore, although law enforcement may be most concerned with the prevention and punishment of crimes, organizations exist to discourage a wide variety of non-criminal violations of rules and norms, effected through the imposition of less severe consequences.
Ruby Ridge	Ruby Ridge was the site of a deadly confrontation and siege in northern Idaho in 1992 between Randy Weaver, his family, Weaver's friend Kevin Harris, and agents of the United States Marshals Service and Federal Bureau of Investigation. It resulted in the death of Weaver's son Sammy, his wife Vicki, and Deputy US Marshal William Francis Degan. At the subsequent federal criminal trial of Weaver and Harris, Weaver's attorney Gerry Spence made accusations of 'criminal wrongdoing' against every agency involved in the incident: the FBI, USMS, the Bureau of Alcohol, Tobacco, Firearms and Explosives (ATF), and the United States Attorney's Office (USAO) for Idaho.

3. Criminal Law

Law commission	A law commission is an independent body set up by a government to conduct law reform; that is, to consider the state of laws in a jurisdiction and make recommendations or proposals for legal changes or restructuring. Their functions include drafting revised versions of confusing laws, preparing consolidated versions of laws, making recommendations on updating outdated laws and making recommendations on repealing obsolete or spent laws. •Australia - Australian Law Reform Commission•Canada - Law Commission of Canada established by the Law Commission of Canada Act on July 1, 1997, replacing the Law Reform Commission of Canada which had been dissolved in 1993 by the Mulroney government.
CrimeStat	CrimeStat is a crime mapping software program. CrimeStat is Windows-based program that conducts spatial and statistical analysis and is designed to interface with a geographic information system (GIS). The program is developed by Ned Levine & Associates, with funding by the National Institute of Justice (NIJ), an agency of the United States Department of Justice.
Procedural law	Procedural law, criminal or administrative proceedings. The rules are designed to ensure a fair and consistent application of due process (in the U.S). or fundamental justice (in other common law countries) to all cases that come before a court.
Christopher Commission	The Independent Commission on the Los Angeles Police Department, informally known as the Christopher Commission, was formed in April 1991, in the wake of the Rodney King beating, by then-mayor of Los Angeles Tom Bradley. It was chaired by attorney Warren Christopher (who later became U.S. Secretary of State under President Bill Clinton). 'The commission was created to conduct 'a full and fair examination of the structure and operation of the LAPD,' including its recruitment and training practices, internal disciplinary system, and citizen complaint system.' However, with the election of Richard Riordan, these reforms were put on hold.
Administrative law	Administrative law is the body of law that governs the activities of administrative agencies of government. Government agency action can include rulemaking, adjudication, or the enforcement of a specific regulatory agenda. Administrative law is considered a branch of public law.
Ponzi scheme	A Ponzi scheme is a fraudulent investment operation that pays returns to its investors from their own money or the money paid by subsequent investors, rather than from profit earned by the individual or organization running the operation. The Ponzi scheme usually entices new investors by offering higher returns than other investments, in the form of short-term returns that are either abnormally high or unusually consistent. Perpetuation of the high returns requires an ever-increasing flow of money from new investors to keep the scheme going.
Speedy trial	The Speedy Trial Clause of the Sixth Amendment to the United States Constitution provides that '[i]n all criminal prosecutions, the accused shall enjoy the right to a speedy . . . trial . . . .' The Clause protects the defendant from delay between the presentation of the indictment or similar charging instrument and the beginning of trial.

Witness protection	Witness protection is protection of a threatened witness or any person involved in the justice system, including defendants and other clients, before, during and after a trial, usually by police. While a witness may only require protection until the conclusion of a trial, some witnesses are provided with a new identity and may live out the rest of their lives under government protection.
	Witness protection is usually required in trials against organized crime, where law enforcement sees a risk for witnesses to be intimidated by colleagues of defendants.
Espionage	Espionage is considered secret or confidential without the permission of the holder of the information. Espionage is inherently clandestine, as it is taken for granted that it is unwelcome and, in many cases illegal and punishable by law. It is a subset of intelligence gathering-which otherwise may be conducted from public sources and using perfectly legal and ethical means.
Inchoate offense	An inchoate offense, inchoate offence, or inchoate crime is a crime of preparing for or seeking to commit another crime. The most common example of an inchoate offense is 'attempt.' 'Inchoate offense' has been defined as 'Conduct deemed criminal without actual harm being done, provided that the harm that would have occurred is one the law tries to prevent.' Intent
	Every inchoate crime or offence must have the mens rea of intent or of recklessness, but most typically intent. Absent a specific law, an inchoate offense requires that the defendant have the specific intent to commit the underlying crime.
Treason	In law, treason is the crime that covers some of the more extreme acts against one's sovereign or nation. Historically, treason also covered the murder of specific social superiors, such as the murder of a husband by his wife. Treason against the king was known as high treason and treason against a lesser superior was petty treason.
Actus reus	Actus reus, is the Latin term for the 'guilty act' which, when proved beyond a reasonable doubt in combination with the mens rea, 'guilty mind', produces criminal liability in the common law-based criminal law jurisdictions of Canada, Australia, India, Pakistan, South Africa, New Zealand, England, Ghana, Wales, Ireland and the United States. In the United States, some crimes also require proof of an attendant circumstance. Etymology
	The terms actus reus and mens rea developed in English Law are derived from the principle stated by Edward Coke, namely, actus non facit reum nisi mens sit rea, which means: 'an act does not make a person guilty unless (their) mind is also guilty'; hence, the general test of guilt is one that requires proof of fault, culpability or blameworthiness both in behaviour and mind.

3. Criminal Law

Community policing	Community policing is a policing strategy and philosophy based on the notion that community interaction and support can help control crime and reduce fear, with community members helping to identify suspects, detain offenders, bring problems to the attention of police, or otherwise target the social problems which give rise to a crime problem in Community policing is a philosophy that promotes organizational strategies that support the systematic use of partnerships and problem-solving techniques, which proactively address the immediate conditions that give rise to public safety issues such as crime, social disorder, and fear of crime. Community Policing consists of three key components: Community Partnerships: Collaborative partnerships between the law enforcement agency and the individuals and organizations they serve to develop solutions to problems and increase trust in police. These partnerships are forged in conjunction with other government agencies,community members and groups, human and social service providers, private businesses, and the media.
Computer fraud	Computer fraud is the use of information technology to commit fraud. In the United States, computer fraud is specifically proscribed by the Computer Fraud and Abuse Act, which provides for jail time and fines. Notable incidentsUnauthorized access at North Bay Abdulswamad Nino Macapayad, a former accounts payable clerk for North Bay Health Care Group, admitted to using her computer to access North Bay's accounting software without authorization, and in turn issued various checks payable to herself and others.
Fraud	In criminal law, a fraud is an intentional deception made for personal gain or to damage another individual; the related adjective is fraudulent. The specific legal definition varies by legal jurisdiction. Fraud is a crime, and also a civil law violation.
Hate crime	In both crime and law, hate crimes (also known as bias-motivated crimes, or a race hate) occur when a perpetrator targets a victim because of his or her perceived membership in a certain social group. Examples of such groups include but are not limited to: racial group, religion, sexual orientation, ethnicity, or gender identity. A hate crime is a category used to describe bias-motivated violence: 'assault, injury, and murder on the basis of certain personal characteristics: different appearance, different color, different nationality, different language, different religion.' 'Hate crime' generally refers to criminal acts that are seen to have been motivated by bias against one or more of the types above, or of their derivatives.
Mortgage fraud	Mortgage fraud is a crime in which the intent is to materially misrepresent or omit information on a mortgage loan application to obtain a loan or to obtain a larger loan than would have been obtained had the lender or borrower known the truth.

In United States federal courts, mortgage fraud is prosecuted as wire fraud, bank fraud, mail fraud and money laundering, with penalties of up to thirty years imprisonment. As the incidence of mortgage fraud has risen over the past few years, states have also begun to enact their own penalties for mortgage fraud.

Criminal negligence	In criminal law, criminal negligence is one of the three general classes of mens rea element required to constitute a conventional as opposed to strict liability offense. It is defined as an act that is:careless, inattentive, neglectful, willfully blind, or in the case of gross negligence what would have been reckless in any other defendant. Concept
	To constitute a crime, there must be an actus reus accompanied by the mens rea . Negligence shows the least level of culpability, intention being the most serious and recklessness of intermediate seriousness, overlapping with gross negligence.
Mens rea	Mens rea is Latin for 'guilty mind'. In criminal law, it is viewed as one of the necessary elements of some crimes. The standard common law test of criminal liability is usually expressed in the Latin phrase, actus non facit reum nisi mens sit rea, which means 'the act does not make a person guilty unless the mind is also guilty'.
Strict liability	In law, strict liability is a standard for liability which may exist in either a criminal or civil context. A rule specifying strict liability makes a person legally responsible for the damage and loss caused by his or her acts and omissions regardless of culpability (including fault in criminal law terms, typically the presence of mens rea). Strict liability is prominent in tort law (especially product liability), corporations law, and criminal law.
Principle of legality	The principle of legality is the legal ideal that requires all law to be clear, ascertainable and non-retrospective. It requires decision makers to resolve disputes by applying legal rules that have been declared beforehand, and not to alter the legal situation retrospectively by discretionary departures from established law. It is closely related to legal formalism and the rule of law and can be traced from the writings of Feuerbach, Dicey and Montesquieu.
Aryan Brotherhood	The Aryan Brotherhood, the AB, Alice Baker, or the One-Two, is a white supremacist prison gang and organized crime syndicate in the United States with about 20,000 members in and out of prison. According to the Federal Bureau of Investigation (FBI), the gang makes up less than 1% of the prison population, but it is responsible for up to 20% of murders in the federal prison system. The AB has focused on the economic activities typical of organized crime entities, particularly drug trafficking, extortion, inmate prostitution, and murder-for-hire.
Mann Act	The White-Slave Traffic Act, better known as the Mann Act, is a United States law, passed June 25, 1910 (ch. 395, 36 Stat. 825; codified as amended at 18 U.S.C. §§ 2421-2424).

Its primary stated intent was to address prostitution, 'immorality', and human trafficking; however, its ambiguous language of 'immorality' allowed selective prosecutions for many years, and was used to criminalize forms of consensual sexual behavior. It was later amended by Congress in 1978, and again in 1986 to apply only to transport for the purpose of prostitution or illegal sexual acts.

Corpus delicti

Corpus delicti is a term from Western jurisprudence referring to the principle that a crime must have been proven to have occurred before a person can be convicted of committing that crime.

For example, a person cannot be tried for larceny unless it can be proven that property has been stolen. Likewise, in order for a person to be tried for arson it must be proven that a criminal act resulted in the burning of a property.

Malice aforethought

Malice aforethought is the 'premeditation' or 'predetermination' that was required as an element of some crimes in some jurisdictions, and a unique element for first-degree or aggravated murder in a few.

Malice aforethought was the mens rea element of murder in 19th-Century America, and remains as a relic in those states with a separate First-degree murder charge.

As of 1891, Texas courts were overwhelmed with discussing whether 'malice' needs to be expressed or implied in the judge's jury instructions.

Manslaughter

Manslaughter is a legal term for the killing of a human being, in a manner considered by law as less culpable than murder. The distinction between murder and manslaughter is said to have first been made by the Ancient Athenian lawmaker Draco in the 7th century BCE.

The definition of manslaughter differs from jurisdiction to jurisdiction. The law generally differentiates between levels of criminal culpability based on the mens rea, or state of mind; or the circumstances under which the killing occurred (mitigating factors).

Alibi

An alibi is a form of defense used in criminal procedure wherein the accused attempts to prove that he or she was in some other place at the time the alleged offense was committed. The Criminal Law Deskbook of Criminal Procedure states: 'Alibi is different from all of the other defenses; it is based upon the premise that the defendant is truly innocent.' In the Latin language alibi means 'somewhere else.'

In some legal jurisdictions there may be a requirement that the accused disclose an alibi defence prior to the trial. This is an exception to the rule that a criminal defendant cannot normally be compelled to furnish information to the prosecution.

Deadly force	Deadly force, as defined by the United States Armed Forces, is the force which a person uses, causing-or that a person knows, or should know, would create a substantial risk of causing-death or serious bodily harm. In most jurisdictions, the use of deadly force is justified only under conditions of extreme necessity as a last resort, when all lesser means have failed or cannot reasonably be employed.
	Firearms, bladed weapons, explosives, and vehicles are among those weapons the use of which is considered deadly force.
Right of self-defense	The right of self-defense (according to U.S. law) (also called, when it applies to the defense of another, alter ego defense, defense of others, defense of a third person) is the right for civilians acting on their own behalf to engage in a level of violence, called reasonable force or defensive force, for the sake of defending one's own life or the lives of others, including, in certain circumstances, the use of deadly force. Theory
	The early theories make no distinction between defense of the person and defense of property. Whether consciously or not, this builds on the Roman Law principle of dominium where any attack on the members of the family or the property it owned was a personal attack on the pater familias - the male head of the household, sole owner of all property belonging to the household, and endowed by law with dominion over all his descendants through the male line no matter their age.
Self-defense	Self-defense or private defense is a countermeasure that involves defending oneself, one's property, or the well-being of another from harm. The use of the right of self-defense as a legal justification for the use of force in times of danger is available in many jurisdictions, but the interpretation varies widely. Physical
	Physical self-defense is the use of physical force to counter an immediate threat of violence.
Probation	Probation developed from the efforts of a philanthropist, John Augustus, who looked for ways to rehabilitate the behavior of criminals. Probation literally means testing of strange behaviour or abilities. In a legal sense, an offender on probation is ordered to follow certain conditions set forth by the court, often under the supervision of a probation officer.
Domestic violence	Domestic violence, spousal abuse, battering, family violence, and intimate partner violence (IPV), is defined as a pattern of abusive behaviors by one partner against another in an intimate relationship such as marriage, dating, family, or cohabitation. Domestic violence, so defined, has many forms, including physical aggression or assault (hitting, kicking, biting, shoving, restraining, slapping, throwing objects), or threats thereof; sexual abuse; emotional abuse; controlling or domineering; intimidation; stalking; passive/covert abuse (e.g., neglect); and economic deprivation.

3. Criminal Law

Duress	In jurisprudence duress refers to a situation whereby a person performs an act as a result of violence, duress, threat or other pressure against the person. Black's Law Dictionary (6th ed). defines duress as 'any unlawful threat or coercion used... to induce another to act [or not act] in a manner [they] otherwise would not [or would]'.
Resisting unlawful arrest	Resisting unlawful arrest is a possible justification for breaking the law. Defendants who use this defense are arguing that they should not be held guilty for a crime, since the actions taken were intended to protect them from an unlawful arrest. Many courts will not tolerate any violence whatsoever (committed while resisting an unlawful arrest), and almost certainly not 'deadly force,' unless the police began to use violence before the defendant began to do so.
Durham rule	The Durham Rule or 'product test' was adopted by the United States Court of Appeals for the District of Columbia Circuit in 1954, in the case of Durham v. U.S. (214 F.2d 862), and states that '... an accused is not criminally responsible if his unlawful act was the product of mental disease or defect'. Durham was later overturned in the case U.S. v. Brawner, 471 F.2d 969 (1972). After the 1970s, U.S. jurisdictions have tended to not recognize this argument as it places emphasis on 'mental disease or defect' and thus on testimony by psychiatrists and is argued to be somewhat ambiguous.
Innocence Protection Act	In United States federal criminal law, the Innocence Protection Act is the first federal death penalty reform to be enacted. The Act seeks to ensure the fair administration of the death penalty and minimize the risk of executing innocent people. The Innocence Protection Act of 2001, introduced in the Senate as S. 486 and the House of Representatives as H.R. 912, was included as Title IV of the omnibus Justice for All Act of 2004 (H.R. 5107), signed into law on October 30, 2004 by President George W. Bush as public law no. 108-405.
Insanity defense	In criminal trials, the insanity defense is where the defendant claims that he or she was not responsible for his or her actions due to mental health problems (psychiatric illness or mental handicap). The exemption of the insane from full criminal punishment dates back to at least the Code of Hammurabi. There are different definitions of legal insanity, such as the M'Naghten Rules, the Durham Rule, the American Legal Institute definition, and various miscellaneous provisions .
Irresistible impulse	In criminal law, irresistible impulse is a defense by excuse, in this case some sort of insanity, in which the defendant argues that they should not be held criminally liable for their actions that broke the law, because they could not control those actions.
	In 1994, Lorena Bobbitt was found not guilty when her defense argued that an irresistible impulse led her to cut off her husband's penis.
	The Penal Code of the U.S. state of California states (2002), 'The defense of diminished capacity is hereby abolished ... there shall be no defense of ... diminished responsibility or irresistible impulse...'

Model Penal Code	The Model Penal Code is a statutory text which was developed by the American Law Institute (ALI) in 1962. The Chief Reporter on the project was Herbert Wechsler. The current form of the Model Penal Code was last updated in 1981. The purpose of the Model Penal Code was to stimulate and assist legislatures in making an effort to update and standardize the penal law of the United States of America. Primary responsibility for criminal law lies with the individual states, and such national efforts work to produce similar laws in different jurisdictions. The standard they used to make a sense of what the penal code should be was one of 'contemporary reasoned judgment' - meaning what a reasoned person at the time of the development of the Model Penal Code would judge the penal law to do.
Jurisdiction	Jurisdiction is the practical authority granted to a formally constituted legal body or to a political leader to deal with and make pronouncements on legal matters and, by implication, to administer justice within a defined area of responsibility. The term is also used to denote the geographical area or subject-matter to which such authority applies. Jurisdiction draws its substance from public international law, conflict of laws, constitutional law and the powers of the executive and legislative branches of government to allocate resources to best serve the needs of its native society.
Insanity Defense Reform Act	The Insanity Defense Reform Act of 1984 was a law passed in the wake of public outrage after John Hinckley, Jr.'s acquittal for the Reagan assassination attempt. It amended the United States federal laws governing defendants with mental diseases or defects to make it significantly more difficult to obtain a verdict of not guilty only by reason of insanity. It was criticized by psychologist Lawrence Z. Freedman for being ineffective: 'If the attacker is rational mentally, stable emotionally, and fanatic politically, he will not be deterred.
Due process	Due process is the legal requirement that the state must respect all of the legal rights that are owed to a person. Due process balances the power of law of the land and protects the individual person from it. When a government harms a person without following the exact course of the law, this constitutes a due-process violation, which offends against the rule of law.
Double Jeopardy	Double jeopardy is a procedural defence that forbids a defendant from being tried again on the same charges following a legitimate acquittal or conviction. In common law countries, a defendant may enter a peremptory plea of autrefois acquit or autrefois convict, meaning the defendant has been acquitted or convicted of the same offence. If this issue is raised, evidence will be placed before the court, which will normally rule as a preliminary matter whether the plea is substantiated, and if it so finds, the projected trial will be prevented from proceeding.
Entrapment	In criminal law, entrapment is constituted by a law enforcement agent inducing a person to commit an offense that the person would otherwise have been unlikely to commit.

3. Criminal Law

	In many jurisdictions, entrapment is a possible defense against criminal liability. However, there is no entrapment where a person is ready and willing to break the law and the government agents merely provide what appears to be a favorable opportunity for the person to commit the crime.
Collateral estoppel	Collateral estoppel, known in modern terminology as issue preclusion, is a common law estoppel doctrine that prevents a person from relitigating an issue. One summary is that 'once a court has decided an issue of fact or law necessary to its judgment, that decision ... preclude[s] relitigation of the issue in a suit on a different cause of action involving a party to the first case.' The rationale behind issue preclusion is the prevention of legal harassment and the prevention of abuse of judicial resources. Issue Parties may be estopped from litigating determinations on issues made in prior actions.
Prosecutorial misconduct	In jurisprudence, prosecutorial misconduct is a procedural defense; via which, a defendant may argue that they should not be held criminally liable for actions which may have broken the law, because the prosecution acted in an 'inappropriate' or 'unfair' manner. Such arguments may involve allegations that the prosecution withheld evidence or knowingly permitted false testimony. This is similar to selective prosecution.

1. The _____, the AB, Alice Baker, or the One-Two, is a white supremacist prison gang and organized crime syndicate in the United States with about 20,000 members in and out of prison. According to the Federal Bureau of Investigation (FBI), the gang makes up less than 1% of the prison population, but it is responsible for up to 20% of murders in the federal prison system. The AB has focused on the economic activities typical of organized crime entities, particularly drug trafficking, extortion, inmate prostitution, and murder-for-hire.

   a. American Front
   b. Necessity
   c. Vicarious liability
   d. Aryan Brotherhood

2. . _____ or private defense is a countermeasure that involves defending oneself, one's property, or the well-being of another from harm. The use of the right of _____ as a legal justification for the use of force in times of danger is available in many jurisdictions, but the interpretation varies widely. Physical

   Physical _____ is the use of physical force to counter an immediate threat of violence.

a. reasonable force
b. reasonable force
c. Castle doctrine
d. Self-defense

3. A _____ is a fraudulent investment operation that pays returns to its investors from their own money or the money paid by subsequent investors, rather than from profit earned by the individual or organization running the operation. The _____ usually entices new investors by offering higher returns than other investments, in the form of short-term returns that are either abnormally high or unusually consistent. Perpetuation of the high returns requires an ever-increasing flow of money from new investors to keep the scheme going.

a. Shell game
b. Ponzi scheme
c. Homeland Security Act
d. Fair and Accurate Credit Transactions Act

4. In criminal trials, the _____ is where the defendant claims that he or she was not responsible for his or her actions due to mental health problems (psychiatric illness or mental handicap). The exemption of the insane from full criminal punishment dates back to at least the Code of Hammurabi. There are different definitions of legal insanity, such as the M'Naghten Rules, the Durham Rule, the American Legal Institute definition, and various miscellaneous provisions .

a. Integrative criminology
b. Investigative psychology
c. Insanity defense
d. UCL Jill Dando Institute

5. _____, criminal or administrative proceedings. The rules are designed to ensure a fair and consistent application of due process (in the U.S) or fundamental justice (in other common law countries) to all cases that come before a court.

a. Procedural law
b. Homeland Security Act
c. Fair and Accurate Credit Transactions Act
d. RAIDS Online

1. d
2. d
3. b
4. c
5. a

You can take the complete Chapter Practice Test

for 3. Criminal Law
on all key terms, persons, places, and concepts.

Online 99 Cents

http://www.epub4670.4.23017.3.cram101.com/

Use www.Cram101.com for all your study needs

including Cram101's online interactive problem solving labs in

chemistry, statistics, mathematics, and more.

4. Policing: Purpose and Organization

Law enforcement

Crime statistics

Appellate court

Crime prevention

CompStat

CrimeStat

Ponzi scheme

Community policing

Domestic violence

Combined DNA Index System

Criminal justice

Speedy trial

Sex Offender

Fusion center

International Police

CAN-SPAM Act

Command hierarchy

Span of control

Intelligence-led policing

Community Oriented Policing Services

Crime control

CHAPTER OUTLINE: KEY TERMS, PEOPLE, PLACES, CONCEPTS

	Violent crime
	Sarbanes-Oxley Act
	Mollen Commission

CHAPTER HIGHLIGHTS & NOTES: KEY TERMS, PEOPLE, PLACES, CONCEPTS

Law enforcement	Law enforcement broadly refers to any system by which some members of society act in an organized manner to promote adherence to the law by discovering and punishing persons who violate the rules and norms governing that society. Although the term may encompass entities such as courts and prisons, it is most frequently applied to those who directly engage in patrols or surveillance to dissuade and discover criminal activity, and those who investigate crimes and apprehend offenders. Furthermore, although law enforcement may be most concerned with the prevention and punishment of crimes, organizations exist to discourage a wide variety of non-criminal violations of rules and norms, effected through the imposition of less severe consequences.
Crime statistics	Crime statistics attempt to provide statistical measures of the crime in societies. Given that crime is usually secretive by nature, measurements of it are likely to be inaccurate.

Several methods for measuring crime exist, including household surveys, hospital or insurance records, and compilations by police and similar law enforcement agencies. |
| Appellate court | An appellate court, commonly called an appeals court or court of appeals or appeal court, is any court of law that is empowered to hear an appeal of a trial court or other lower tribunal. In most jurisdictions, the court system is divided into at least three levels: the trial court, which initially hears cases and reviews evidence and testimony to determine the facts of the case; at least one intermediate appellate court; and a supreme court which primarily reviews the decisions of the intermediate courts. A jurisdiction's supreme court is that jurisdiction's highest appellate court. |
| Crime prevention | Crime prevention is the attempt to reduce victimization and to deter crime and criminals. It is applied specifically to efforts made by governments to reduce crime, enforce the law, and maintain criminal justice. |

4. Policing: Purpose and Organization

CompStat	CompStat--or COMPSTAT--(short for COMPuter STATistics or COMParative STATistics) is the name given to the New York City Police Department's accountability process and has since been replicated in many other departments. CompStat is a management philosophy or organizational management tool for police departments, roughly equivalent to Six Sigma or TQM, and is not a computer system or software package. Instead, CompStat is a multilayered dynamic approach to crime reduction, quality of life improvement, and personnel and resource management.
CrimeStat	CrimeStat is a crime mapping software program. CrimeStat is Windows-based program that conducts spatial and statistical analysis and is designed to interface with a geographic information system (GIS). The program is developed by Ned Levine & Associates, with funding by the National Institute of Justice (NIJ), an agency of the United States Department of Justice.
Ponzi scheme	A Ponzi scheme is a fraudulent investment operation that pays returns to its investors from their own money or the money paid by subsequent investors, rather than from profit earned by the individual or organization running the operation. The Ponzi scheme usually entices new investors by offering higher returns than other investments, in the form of short-term returns that are either abnormally high or unusually consistent. Perpetuation of the high returns requires an ever-increasing flow of money from new investors to keep the scheme going.
Community policing	Community policing is a policing strategy and philosophy based on the notion that community interaction and support can help control crime and reduce fear, with community members helping to identify suspects, detain offenders, bring problems to the attention of police, or otherwise target the social problems which give rise to a crime problem in Community policing is a philosophy that promotes organizational strategies that support the systematic use of partnerships and problem-solving techniques, which proactively address the immediate conditions that give rise to public safety issues such as crime, social disorder, and fear of crime. Community Policing consists of three key components: Community Partnerships: Collaborative partnerships between the law enforcement agency and the individuals and organizations they serve to develop solutions to problems and increase trust in police. These partnerships are forged in conjunction with other government agencies,community members and groups, human and social service providers, private businesses, and the media.
Domestic violence	Domestic violence, spousal abuse, battering, family violence, and intimate partner violence (IPV), is defined as a pattern of abusive behaviors by one partner against another in an intimate relationship such as marriage, dating, family, or cohabitation. Domestic violence, so defined, has many forms, including physical aggression or assault (hitting, kicking, biting, shoving, restraining, slapping, throwing objects), or threats thereof; sexual abuse; emotional abuse; controlling or domineering; intimidation; stalking; passive/covert abuse (e.g., neglect); and economic deprivation.

4. Policing: Purpose and Organization

Combined DNA Index System	The Combined DNA Index System is a DNA database funded by the United States Federal Bureau of Investigation (FBI). It is a computer system that stores DNA profiles created by federal, state, and local crime laboratories in the United States, with the ability to search the database to assist in the identification of suspects in crimes. Origins CODIS was an outgrowth of the Technical Working Group on DNA Analysis Methods (TWGDAM, now SWGDAM) which developed guidelines for standards of practice in the United States and Canadian crime laboratories as they began DNA testing in the late 1980s.
Criminal justice	Criminal justice is the system of practices and institutions of governments directed at upholding social control, deterring and mitigating crime, or sanctioning those who violate laws with criminal penalties and rehabilitation efforts. Those accused of crime have protections against abuse of investigatory and prosecution powers. Goals In the United States, criminal justice policy has been guided by the 1967 President's Commission on Law Enforcement and Administration of Justice, which issued a ground-breaking report 'The Challenge of Crime in a Free Society'.
Speedy trial	The Speedy Trial Clause of the Sixth Amendment to the United States Constitution provides that '[i]n all criminal prosecutions, the accused shall enjoy the right to a speedy . . . trial . . . .' The Clause protects the defendant from delay between the presentation of the indictment or similar charging instrument and the beginning of trial.
Sex Offender	A sex offender is a person who has committed a sex crime or in some instances even mere public urination. What constitutes a sex crime differs by culture and legal jurisdiction. Most jurisdictions compile their laws into sections, such as traffic, assault and sexual.
Fusion center	A fusion center is an information sharing center, many of which were jointly created between 2003 and 2007 under the U.S. Department of Homeland Security and the Office of Justice Programs in the U.S. Department of Justice. They are designed to promote information sharing at the federal level between agencies such as the Central Intelligence Agency (CIA), Federal Bureau of Investigation (FBI), U.S. Department of Justice, U.S. military, and state- and local-level government. As of July 2009, the U.S. Department of Homeland Security recognized at least 72 fusion centers.
International Police	The International Police is the title used for an organization of police officers representing various countries throughout the world, brought together to assist in the training, organization, stabilization of a destabilized region, or creation of indigenous police forces primarily in war-torn countries. It should not be confused with Interpol, which is a different organization.

4. Policing: Purpose and Organization

CAN-SPAM Act	The CAN-SPAM Act of 2003 (15 U.S.C. 7701, et seq., Public Law No. 108-187, was S.877 of the 108th United States Congress), signed into law by President George W. Bush on December 16, 2003, establishes the United States' first national standards for the sending of commercial e-mail and requires the Federal Trade Commission (FTC) to enforce its provisions. The acronym CAN-SPAM derives from the bill's full name: Controlling the Assault of Non-Solicited Pornography And Marketing Act of 2003. This is also a play on the usual term for unsolicited email of this type, spam. The bill was sponsored in Congress by Senators Conrad Burns and Ron Wyden.
Command hierarchy	A command hierarchy is a group of people dedicated to carrying out orders 'from the top', that is, of authority. It is part of a power structure: usually seen as the most vulnerable and also the most powerful part of it.
Span of control	Span of control is the term now used more commonly in business management, particularly human resource management. Span of control refers to the number of subordinates a supervisor has. In the hierarchical business organization of some time in the past it was not uncommon to see average spans of 1 to 4 or even less.
Intelligence-led policing	Intelligence-led policing is a policing model that has emerged in recent years which is 'built around risk assessment and risk management.' Although there is no universally accepted understanding of what intelligence-led policing entails, the leading definition is that intelligence\ led\ policing is 'a strategic, future-oriented and targeted approach to crime control, focusing upon the identification, analysis and 'management' of persisting and developing 'problems' or 'risks.' In simpler terms, 'it is a model of policing in which intelligence serves as a guide to operations, rather than the reverse. Calls for intelligence-led policing originated in the 1990s, both in Britain and in the United States. In the U.S. Mark Riebling's 1994 book Wedge - The Secret War between the FBI and CIA spotlighted the conflict between law enforcement and intelligence, and urged cops to become 'more like spies.' Intelligence-led policing gained considerable momentum globally following the September 11 terrorist attacks on the United States.
Community Oriented Policing Services	The Office of Community Oriented Policing Services is an agency within the United States Department of Justice. Community Oriented Policing Services was established through a provision in the 1994 Violent Crime Control and Law Enforcement Act. Since 1994, Community Oriented Policing Services has provided $11.3 billion in assistance to state and local law enforcement agencies to help in hiring additional police officers.
Crime control	Crime control refers to methods taken to reduce crime in a society.

Penology often focuses on the use of criminal penalties as a means of deterring people from committing crimes and temporarily or permanently incapacitating those who have already committed crimes from re-offending. Crime prevention is also widely implemented in some countries, through government police and, in many cases, private policing methods such as private security and home defense.

Violent crime	A violent crime is a crime in which the offender uses or threatens to use violent force upon the victim. This entails both crimes in which the violent act is the objective, such as murder, as well as crimes in which violence is the means to an end, (including criminal ends) such as robbery. Violent crimes include crimes committed with weapons.
Sarbanes-Oxley Act	The Sarbanes-Oxley Act of 2002, also known as the 'Public Company Accounting Reform and Investor Protection Act' (in the Senate) and 'Corporate and Auditing Accountability and Responsibility Act' (in the House) and more commonly called Sarbanes-Oxley, Sarbox or SOX, is a United States federal law that set new or enhanced standards for all U.S. public company boards, management and public accounting firms. S. Senator Paul Sarbanes (D-MD) and U.S. Representative Michael G. Oxley (R-OH). As a result of SOX, top management must now individually certify the accuracy of financial information.
Mollen Commission	The Mollen Commission is formally known as The City of New York Commission to Investigate Allegations of Police Corruption and the Anti-Corruption Procedures of the Police Department. Former judge Milton Mollen was appointed in July 1992 by then New York City mayor David N. Dinkins to investigate corruption in the New York City Police Department. Mollen's mandate was to examine and investigate 'the nature and extent of corruption in the Department; evaluate the departments procedures for preventing and detecting that corruption; and recommend changes and improvements to those procedures'.

CHAPTER QUIZ: KEY TERMS, PEOPLE, PLACES, CONCEPTS

1. The Office of _____ is an agency within the United States Department of Justice. _____ was established through a provision in the 1994 Violent Crime Control and Law Enforcement Act. Since 1994, _____ has provided $11.3 billion in assistance to state and local law enforcement agencies to help in hiring additional police officers.

   a. computer trespass
   b. Community Oriented Policing Services
   c. Fair and Accurate Credit Transactions Act
   d. Social control

2. . _____ is the term now used more commonly in business management, particularly human resource management. _____ refers to the number of subordinates a supervisor has.

In the hierarchical business organization of some time in the past it was not uncommon to see average spans of 1 to 4 or even less.

a. Span of control
b. Homeland Security Act
c. Fair and Accurate Credit Transactions Act
d. Social control

3. The _____ Clause of the Sixth Amendment to the United States Constitution provides that '[i]n all criminal prosecutions, the accused shall enjoy the right to a speedy . . . trial . . . .' The Clause protects the defendant from delay between the presentation of the indictment or similar charging instrument and the beginning of trial.

a. Speedy trial
b. Homeland Security Act
c. Fair and Accurate Credit Transactions Act
d. Prison Rape Elimination Act

4. A _____ is a fraudulent investment operation that pays returns to its investors from their own money or the money paid by subsequent investors, rather than from profit earned by the individual or organization running the operation. The _____ usually entices new investors by offering higher returns than other investments, in the form of short-term returns that are either abnormally high or unusually consistent. Perpetuation of the high returns requires an ever-increasing flow of money from new investors to keep the scheme going.

a. Shell game
b. Black money scam
c. Ponzi scheme
d. RAIDS Online

5. _____ broadly refers to any system by which some members of society act in an organized manner to promote adherence to the law by discovering and punishing persons who violate the rules and norms governing that society. Although the term may encompass entities such as courts and prisons, it is most frequently applied to those who directly engage in patrols or surveillance to dissuade and discover criminal activity, and those who investigate crimes and apprehend offenders. Furthermore, although _____ may be most concerned with the prevention and punishment of crimes, organizations exist to discourage a wide variety of non-criminal violations of rules and norms, effected through the imposition of less severe consequences.

a. Background check
b. Law enforcement
c. Campus police
d. Counter-terrorism

1. b

2. a

3. a

4. c

5. b

You can take the complete Chapter Practice Test

for 4. Policing: Purpose and Organization
on all key terms, persons, places, and concepts.

Online 99 Cents

http://www.epub4670.4.23017.4.cram101.com/

Use www.Cram101.com for all your study needs

including Cram101's online interactive problem solving labs in

chemistry, statistics, mathematics, and more.

CHAPTER OUTLINE: KEY TERMS, PEOPLE, PLACES, CONCEPTS

	Contagious shooting
	CAN-SPAM Act
	Due process
	Identity theft
	Sarbanes-Oxley Act
	Deadly force
	Exclusionary rule
	Search and seizure
	Criminal justice
	Fourth Amendment
	Ponzi scheme
	Certiorari
	Probable cause
	Plain view
	Law enforcement
	Miranda warning
	Appellate court
	Community policing
	Reasonable suspicion
	Narcotic
	Mortgage fraud

Hate crime

Texas Syndicate

Forward looking infrared

Intellectual Property

Informant

Interrogation

Crime control

Communications Assistance for Law Enforcement Act

Electronic Communication Privacy Act

Mexican Mafia

Surveillance

Computer fraud

Fraud

Crime scene

Electronic evidence

Certified first responder

Contagious shooting	A contagious shooting is a sociological phenomenon observed in military and police personnel in which one person firing on a target can induce others to begin shooting. Often the subsequent shooters will not know why they are firing.

This is defined as 'officers firing because others are doing so,' or according to Professor Eugene J. O'Donnell of John Jay College, 'cops shoot because other cops shoot.' While commonly accepted in popular culture and police jargon, there has been yet no scientific evidence 'to prove the existence of a contagious shooting dynamic,' which O'Donnell said was a 'debateable notion.'

In classic cases involving contagious shooting, 'a gun was shot before any officers fired,' and thus 'the officers involved began shooting because of fear or because of the sound of a colleague firing.'Incidents •2011: On Memorial Day in Miami Beach several police officers fired til empty on a stopped car after the driver smashed into other cars, killing the driver and injuring seven bystanders.•2010: Five cops fired 40 shots at a robbery suspect after carjacking a woman and her two children, killing the suspect and wounding the carjack victims in Jacksonville, Florida.•2010: A bystander was injured in Harlem when a man 'open[ed] fire on responding officers, who fired 46 times in response.' 'In the Harlem episode, unlike the Bell and Diallo cases, a gun was shot before any officers fired, according to the police account. |
| CAN-SPAM Act | The CAN-SPAM Act of 2003 (15 U.S.C. 7701, et seq., Public Law No. 108-187, was S.877 of the 108th United States Congress), signed into law by President George W. Bush on December 16, 2003, establishes the United States' first national standards for the sending of commercial e-mail and requires the Federal Trade Commission (FTC) to enforce its provisions.

The acronym CAN-SPAM derives from the bill's full name: Controlling the Assault of Non-Solicited Pornography And Marketing Act of 2003. This is also a play on the usual term for unsolicited email of this type, spam. The bill was sponsored in Congress by Senators Conrad Burns and Ron Wyden. |
| Due process | Due process is the legal requirement that the state must respect all of the legal rights that are owed to a person. Due process balances the power of law of the land and protects the individual person from it. When a government harms a person without following the exact course of the law, this constitutes a due-process violation, which offends against the rule of law. |
| Identity theft | Identity theft is a form of fraud or cheating of another person's identity in which someone pretends to be someone else by assuming that person's identity, typically in order to access resources or obtain credit and other benefits in that person's name. The victim of identity theft can suffer adverse consequences if he or she is held accountable for the perpetrator's actions. Organizations and individuals who are duped or defrauded by the identity thief can also suffer adverse consequences and losses, and to that extent are also victims. |

5. Policing: Legal Aspects

Sarbanes-Oxley Act	The Sarbanes-Oxley Act of 2002, also known as the 'Public Company Accounting Reform and Investor Protection Act' (in the Senate) and 'Corporate and Auditing Accountability and Responsibility Act' (in the House) and more commonly called Sarbanes-Oxley, Sarbox or SOX, is a United States federal law that set new or enhanced standards for all U.S. public company boards, management and public accounting firms. S. Senator Paul Sarbanes (D-MD) and U.S. Representative Michael G. Oxley (R-OH). As a result of SOX, top management must now individually certify the accuracy of financial information.
Deadly force	Deadly force, as defined by the United States Armed Forces, is the force which a person uses, causing-or that a person knows, or should know, would create a substantial risk of causing-death or serious bodily harm. In most jurisdictions, the use of deadly force is justified only under conditions of extreme necessity as a last resort, when all lesser means have failed or cannot reasonably be employed. Firearms, bladed weapons, explosives, and vehicles are among those weapons the use of which is considered deadly force.
Exclusionary rule	The exclusionary rule is a legal principle in the United States, under constitutional law, which holds that evidence collected or analyzed in violation of the defendant's constitutional rights is sometimes inadmissible for a criminal prosecution in a court of law. This may be considered an example of a prophylactic rule formulated by the judiciary in order to protect a constitutional right. However, in some circumstances at least, the exclusionary rule may also be considered to follow directly from the constitutional language, such as the Fifth Amendment's command that no person 'shall be compelled in any criminal case to be a witness against himself' and that no person 'shall be deprived of life, liberty or property without due process of law'.
Search and seizure	Search and seizure is a legal procedure used in many civil law and common law legal systems whereby police or other authorities and their agents, who suspect that a crime has been committed, do a search of a person's property and confiscate any relevant evidence to the crime. Some countries have provisions in their constitutions that provide the public with the right to be free from 'unreasonable' search and seizure. This right is generally based on the premise that everyone is entitled to a reasonable right to privacy.
Criminal justice	Criminal justice is the system of practices and institutions of governments directed at upholding social control, deterring and mitigating crime, or sanctioning those who violate laws with criminal penalties and rehabilitation efforts. Those accused of crime have protections against abuse of investigatory and prosecution powers. Goals

Fourth Amendment	The Fourth Amendment (Amendment IV) to the United States Constitution is the part of the Bill of Rights which guards against unreasonable searches and seizures, along with requiring any warrant to be judicially sanctioned and supported by probable cause. It was adopted as a response to the abuse of the writ of assistance, which is a type of general search warrant, in the American Revolution. Search and seizure (including arrest) should be limited in scope according to specific information supplied to the issuing court, usually by a law enforcement officer, who has sworn by it. The Fourth Amendment applies to the states by way of the Due Process Clause of the Fourteenth Amendment.
Ponzi scheme	A Ponzi scheme is a fraudulent investment operation that pays returns to its investors from their own money or the money paid by subsequent investors, rather than from profit earned by the individual or organization running the operation. The Ponzi scheme usually entices new investors by offering higher returns than other investments, in the form of short-term returns that are either abnormally high or unusually consistent. Perpetuation of the high returns requires an ever-increasing flow of money from new investors to keep the scheme going.
Certiorari	Certiorari is a type of writ seeking judicial review, recognized in U.S., Roman, English, Canadian, Philippine, and other law, meaning an order by a higher court directing a lower court, tribunal, or public authority to send the record in a given case for review. Certiorari is the present passive infinitive of the Latin verb certiorare ('to inform, apprise, show').
Probable cause	In United States criminal law, probable cause is the standard by which an officer or agent of the law has the grounds to make an arrest, to conduct a personal or property search, or to obtain a warrant for arrest, etc. when criminal charges are being considered. It is also used to refer to the standard to which a grand jury believes that a crime has been committed.
Plain view	The plain view doctrine allows an officer to seize - without a warrant - evidence and contraband found in plain view during a lawful observation. This doctrine is also regularly used by TSA Federal Government Officers while screening persons and property at U.S. airports. For the plain view doctrine to apply for discoveries, the three-prong Horton test requires:•the officer to be lawfully present at the place where the evidence can be plainly viewed,•the officer to have a lawful right of access to the object, and•the incriminating character of the object to be 'immediately apparent.' In order for the officer to seize the item, the officer must have probable cause to believe the item is evidence of a crime or is contraband.
Law enforcement	Law enforcement broadly refers to any system by which some members of society act in an organized manner to promote adherence to the law by discovering and punishing persons who violate the rules and norms governing that society.

Although the term may encompass entities such as courts and prisons, it is most frequently applied to those who directly engage in patrols or surveillance to dissuade and discover criminal activity, and those who investigate crimes and apprehend offenders. Furthermore, although law enforcement may be most concerned with the prevention and punishment of crimes, organizations exist to discourage a wide variety of non-criminal violations of rules and norms, effected through the imposition of less severe consequences.

Miranda warning

The Miranda warning is a warning that is required to be given by police in the United States to criminal suspects in police custody (or in a custodial interrogation) before they are interrogated to inform them about their constitutional rights. In Miranda v. Arizona, the Supreme Court of the United States held that an elicited incriminating statement by a suspect will not constitute admissible evidence unless the suspect was informed of the right to decline to make self-incriminatory statements and the right to legal counsel (hence the so-called 'Miranda rights'), and makes a knowing, intelligent and voluntary waiver of those rights. The Miranda warning is not a condition of detention, but rather a safeguard against self-incrimination; as a result, if law enforcement officials decline to offer a Miranda warning to an individual in their custody, they may still interrogate that person and act upon the knowledge gained, but may not use that person's statements to incriminate him or her in a criminal trial.

Appellate court

An appellate court, commonly called an appeals court or court of appeals or appeal court, is any court of law that is empowered to hear an appeal of a trial court or other lower tribunal. In most jurisdictions, the court system is divided into at least three levels: the trial court, which initially hears cases and reviews evidence and testimony to determine the facts of the case; at least one intermediate appellate court; and a supreme court which primarily reviews the decisions of the intermediate courts. A jurisdiction's supreme court is that jurisdiction's highest appellate court.

Community policing

Community policing is a policing strategy and philosophy based on the notion that community interaction and support can help control crime and reduce fear, with community members helping to identify suspects, detain offenders, bring problems to the attention of police, or otherwise target the social problems which give rise to a crime problem in Community policing is a philosophy that promotes organizational strategies that support the systematic use of partnerships and problem-solving techniques, which proactively address the immediate conditions that give rise to public safety issues such as crime, social disorder, and fear of crime.

Community Policing consists of three key components:

Community Partnerships: Collaborative partnerships between the law enforcement agency and the individuals and organizations they serve to develop solutions to problems and increase trust in police. These partnerships are forged in conjunction with other government agencies,community members and groups, human and social service providers, private businesses, and the media.

Reasonable suspicion	Reasonable suspicion is a legal standard of proof in United States law that is less than probable cause, the legal standard for arrests and warrants, but more than an 'inchoate and unparticularized suspicion or 'hunch'?'; it must be based on 'specific and articulable facts', 'taken together with rational inferences from those facts'. Police may briefly detain a person if they have reasonable suspicion that the person has been, is, or is about to be engaged in criminal activity; such a detention is known as a Terry stop. If police additionally have reasonable suspicion that a person so detained may be armed, they may 'frisk' the person for weapons, but not for contraband like drugs.
Narcotic	The term narcotic originally referred medically to any psychoactive compound with any sleep-inducing properties. In the United States of America it has since become associated with opioids, commonly morphine and heroin and their derivatives, such as hydrocodone. The term is, today, imprecisely defined and typically has negative connotations.
Mortgage fraud	Mortgage fraud is a crime in which the intent is to materially misrepresent or omit information on a mortgage loan application to obtain a loan or to obtain a larger loan than would have been obtained had the lender or borrower known the truth. In United States federal courts, mortgage fraud is prosecuted as wire fraud, bank fraud, mail fraud and money laundering, with penalties of up to thirty years imprisonment. As the incidence of mortgage fraud has risen over the past few years, states have also begun to enact their own penalties for mortgage fraud.
Hate crime	In both crime and law, hate crimes (also known as bias-motivated crimes, or a race hate) occur when a perpetrator targets a victim because of his or her perceived membership in a certain social group. Examples of such groups include but are not limited to: racial group, religion, sexual orientation, ethnicity, or gender identity. A hate crime is a category used to describe bias-motivated violence: 'assault, injury, and murder on the basis of certain personal characteristics: different appearance, different color, different nationality, different language, different religion.' 'Hate crime' generally refers to criminal acts that are seen to have been motivated by bias against one or more of the types above, or of their derivatives.
Texas Syndicate	The Texas Syndicate is a mostly Texas-based prison gang that includes Hispanic and at one time, White (non-Hispanic) members. The Texas Syndicate, unlike La Eme or Nuestra Familia, has been more associated or allied with Mexican immigrant prisoners, known as 'border brothers', while La Eme and the NF tend to be more composed of US-born/raised Hispanics.

5. Policing: Legal Aspects

Forward looking infrared	Forward looking infrared cameras, typically used on military aircraft, use an imaging technology that senses infrared radiation.
	The sensors installed in forward-looking infrared cameras-as well as those of other thermal imaging cameras-use detection of infrared radiation, typically emitted from a heat source, to create a 'picture' assembled for video output. They can be used to help pilots and drivers steer their vehicles at night and in fog, or to detect warm objects against a cooler background.
Intellectual Property	Intellectual property is a legal concept which refers to creations of the mind for which exclusive rights are recognized. Under intellectual property law, owners are granted certain exclusive rights to a variety of intangible assets, such as musical, literary, and artistic works; discoveries and inventions; and words, phrases, symbols, and designs. Common types of intellectual property rights include copyright, trademarks, patents, industrial design rights, trade dress, and in some jurisdictions trade secrets.
Informant	An informant is a person who provides privileged information about a person or organization to an agency. The term is usually used within the law enforcement world, where they are officially known as confidential or criminal informants (CI), and can often refer pejoratively to the supply of information without the consent of the other parties with the intent of malicious, personal or financial gain. However, the term is used in politics, industry and academia.
Interrogation	Interrogation is interviewing as commonly employed by officers of the police, military, and Intelligence agencies with the goal of extracting a confession or obtaining information. Subjects of interrogation are often the suspects, victims, or witnesses of a crime. Interrogation may involve a diverse array of techniques, ranging from developing a rapport with the subject to outright torture.
Crime control	Crime control refers to methods taken to reduce crime in a society. Penology often focuses on the use of criminal penalties as a means of deterring people from committing crimes and temporarily or permanently incapacitating those who have already committed crimes from re-offending. Crime prevention is also widely implemented in some countries, through government police and, in many cases, private policing methods such as private security and home defense.
Communications Assistance for Law Enforcement Act	The Communications Assistance for Law Enforcement Act (CALEA) is a United States wiretapping law passed in 1994, during the presidency of Bill Clinton (Pub. L. No. 103-414, 108 Stat. 4279, codified at 47 USC 1001-1010).

Electronic Communication Privacy Act	Electronic Communication Privacy Act of 1986 was enacted by the United States Congress to extend government restrictions on wire taps from telephone calls to include transmissions of electronic data by computer. Specifically, Electronic Communication Privacy Act was an amendment to Title III of the Omnibus Crime Control and Safe Streets Act of 1968 (the Wiretap Statute), which was primarily designed to prevent unauthorized government access to private electronic communications.
	The Electronic Communication Privacy Act also added new provisions prohibiting access to stored electronic communications, i.e., the Stored Communications Act, 18 U.S.C. §§ 2701-12. The Electronic Communication Privacy Act also included so-called pen/trap provisions that permit the tracing of telephone communications.
Mexican Mafia	The Mexican Mafia, is a Mexican American highly-organized, ruthless crime organization in the United States. Despite its name, the Mexican Mafia did not originate in Mexico and is entirely a U.S. criminal prison organization. Sureños, including MS-13 and Florencia 13, use the number 13 to show allegiance to the Mexican Mafia.
Surveillance	Surveillance is the monitoring of the behavior, activities, or other changing information, usually of people for the purpose of influencing, managing, directing, or protecting. Surveillance is therefore an ambiguous practice, sometimes creating positive effects, at other times negative. It is sometimes done in a surreptitious manner.
Computer fraud	Computer fraud is the use of information technology to commit fraud. In the United States, computer fraud is specifically proscribed by the Computer Fraud and Abuse Act, which provides for jail time and fines. Notable incidentsUnauthorized access at North Bay
	Abdulswamad Nino Macapayad, a former accounts payable clerk for North Bay Health Care Group, admitted to using her computer to access North Bay's accounting software without authorization, and in turn issued various checks payable to herself and others.
Fraud	In criminal law, a fraud is an intentional deception made for personal gain or to damage another individual; the related adjective is fraudulent. The specific legal definition varies by legal jurisdiction. Fraud is a crime, and also a civil law violation.
Crime scene	A crime scene is a location where a crime took place, and comprises the area from which most of the physical evidence is retrieved by law enforcement personnel, crime scene investigators (CSIs) or in rare circumstances, forensic scientists. Evidence collection
	A crime scene is not necessarily where the crime was committed. Indeed, there are primary, secondary and often tertiary crime scenes.

5. Policing: Legal Aspects

Electronic evidence	Digital evidence or electronic evidence is any probative information stored or transmitted in digital form that a party to a court case may use at trial. Before accepting digital evidence a court will determine if the evidence is relevant, whether it is authentic, if it is hearsay and whether a copy is acceptable or the original is required. The use of digital evidence has increased in the past few decades as courts have allowed the use of e-mails, digital photographs, ATM transaction logs, word processing documents, instant message histories, files saved from accounting programs, spreadsheets, internet browser histories, databases, the contents of computer memory, computer backups, computer printouts, Global Positioning System tracks, logs from a hotel's electronic door locks, and digital video or audio files.
Certified first responder	A certified first responder is a person who has completed a course and received certification in providing pre-hospital care for medical emergencies. They have more skill than someone who is trained in basic first aid but they are not a substitute for advanced medical care rendered by emergency medical technicians (EMTs), emergency physicians, nurses, or paramedics. First responder courses cover cardiopulmonary resuscitation (CPR), automated external defibrillator usage, spinal and bone fracture immobilization, oxygen and, in some cases, emergency childbirth as well as advanced first aid.

1. The _____ is a legal principle in the United States, under constitutional law, which holds that evidence collected or analyzed in violation of the defendant's constitutional rights is sometimes inadmissible for a criminal prosecution in a court of law. This may be considered an example of a prophylactic rule formulated by the judiciary in order to protect a constitutional right. However, in some circumstances at least, the _____ may also be considered to follow directly from the constitutional language, such as the Fifth Amendment's command that no person 'shall be compelled in any criminal case to be a witness against himself' and that no person 'shall be deprived of life, liberty or property without due process of law'.

    a. Estoppel
    b. Eminent domain
    c. Exclusionary rule
    d. Open fields doctrine

2. . The _____ of 2002, also known as the 'Public Company Accounting Reform and Investor Protection Act' (in the Senate) and 'Corporate and Auditing Accountability and Responsibility Act' (in the House) and more commonly called Sarbanes-Oxley, Sarbox or SOX, is a United States federal law that set new or enhanced standards for all U.S. public company boards, management and public accounting firms. S. Senator Paul Sarbanes (D-MD) and U.S. Representative Michael G. Oxley (R-OH). As a result of SOX, top management must now individually certify the accuracy of financial information.

a. Second Chance Act
b. Securities Exchange Act of 1934
c. Sarbanes-Oxley Act
d. Speedy Trial Act

3. _____ is a policing strategy and philosophy based on the notion that community interaction and support can help control crime and reduce fear, with community members helping to identify suspects, detain offenders, bring problems to the attention of police, or otherwise target the social problems which give rise to a crime problem in _____ is a philosophy that promotes organizational strategies that support the systematic use of partnerships and problem-solving techniques, which proactively address the immediate conditions that give rise to public safety issues such as crime, social disorder, and fear of crime.

_____ consists of three key components:

Community Partnerships: Collaborative partnerships between the law enforcement agency and the individuals and organizations they serve to develop solutions to problems and increase trust in police. These partnerships are forged in conjunction with other government agencies,community members and groups, human and social service providers, private businesses, and the media.

a. Community policing
b. Bylaw enforcement officer
c. Campus police
d. Counter-terrorism

4. . A _____ is a sociological phenomenon observed in military and police personnel in which one person firing on a target can induce others to begin shooting. Often the subsequent shooters will not know why they are firing.

This is defined as 'officers firing because others are doing so,' or according to Professor Eugene J. O'Donnell of John Jay College, 'cops shoot because other cops shoot.' While commonly accepted in popular culture and police jargon, there has been yet no scientific evidence 'to prove the existence of a _____ dynamic,' which O'Donnell said was a 'debateable notion.'

In classic cases involving _____, 'a gun was shot before any officers fired,' and thus 'the officers involved began shooting because of fear or because of the sound of a colleague firing.'Incidents •2011: On Memorial Day in Miami Beach several police officers fired til empty on a stopped car after the driver smashed into other cars, killing the driver and injuring seven bystanders.•2010: Five cops fired 40 shots at a robbery suspect after carjacking a woman and her two children, killing the suspect and wounding the carjack victims in Jacksonville, Florida.•2010: A bystander was injured in Harlem when a man 'open[ed] fire on responding officers, who fired 46 times in response.' 'In the Harlem episode, unlike the Bell and Diallo cases, a gun was shot before any officers fired, according to the police account.

a. Contempt of cop
b. Crime Information Center

c. Contagious shooting

d. Crisis negotiation

5. _____ is the use of information technology to commit fraud. In the United States, _____ is specifically proscribed by the _____ and Abuse Act, which provides for jail time and fines. Notable incidentsUnauthorized access at North Bay

Abdulswamad Nino Macapayad, a former accounts payable clerk for North Bay Health Care Group, admitted to using her computer to access North Bay's accounting software without authorization, and in turn issued various checks payable to herself and others.

a. Homeland Security Act

b. Targeted Killing in International Law

c. Computer fraud

d. Treason

ANSWER KEY
5. Policing: Legal Aspects

1. c
2. c
3. a
4. c
5. c

You can take the complete Chapter Practice Test

for 5. Policing: Legal Aspects
on all key terms, persons, places, and concepts.

Online 99 Cents

http://www.epub4670.4.23017.5.cram101.com/

Use www.Cram101.com for all your study needs

including Cram101's online interactive problem solving labs in

chemistry, statistics, mathematics, and more.

	Mollen Commission
	Hate crime
	Knapp Commission
	Probation
	Differential association
	Law enforcement
	Domestic violence
	CAN-SPAM Act
	Joint Terrorism Task Force
	Criminal intelligence
	Intelligence-led policing
	Information sharing
	Christopher Commission
	Lawsuit
	Fourth Amendment
	Due process
	Principle of legality
	Community policing
	Racial profiling
	Deadly force
	Ruby Ridge

	Taser
	Suicide
	Suicide by cop
	Durham rule
	Criminal justice
	National Commission on Law Observance and Enforcement
	Witness protection

CHAPTER HIGHLIGHTS & NOTES: KEY TERMS, PEOPLE, PLACES, CONCEPTS

Mollen Commission	The Mollen Commission is formally known as The City of New York Commission to Investigate Allegations of Police Corruption and the Anti-Corruption Procedures of the Police Department. Former judge Milton Mollen was appointed in July 1992 by then New York City mayor David N. Dinkins to investigate corruption in the New York City Police Department. Mollen's mandate was to examine and investigate 'the nature and extent of corruption in the Department; evaluate the departments procedures for preventing and detecting that corruption; and recommend changes and improvements to those procedures'.
Hate crime	In both crime and law, hate crimes (also known as bias-motivated crimes, or a race hate) occur when a perpetrator targets a victim because of his or her perceived membership in a certain social group. Examples of such groups include but are not limited to: racial group, religion, sexual orientation, ethnicity, or gender identity. A hate crime is a category used to describe bias-motivated violence: 'assault, injury, and murder on the basis of certain personal characteristics: different appearance, different color, different nationality, different language, different religion.' 'Hate crime' generally refers to criminal acts that are seen to have been motivated by bias against one or more of the types above, or of their derivatives.

Knapp Commission	The Knapp Commission stemmed from a five-member panel initially formed in April 1970 by Mayor John V. Lindsay to investigate corruption within the New York City Police Department. The creation of the commission was largely a result of the publicity generated by the public revelations of police corruption made by Patrolman Frank Serpico and Sergeant David Durk. Investigation and public hearings
	While the Knapp Commission began its investigation of corruption in the police department in June 1970, public hearings didn't start until October 18, 1971. In addition to the testimony of lamplighters Serpico and Durk, testimony from dozens of other witnesses, including former Police Commissioner Howard R. Leary, corrupt patrolmen and the victims of police shakedowns, were heard.
Probation	Probation developed from the efforts of a philanthropist, John Augustus, who looked for ways to rehabilitate the behavior of criminals. Probation literally means testing of strange behaviour or abilities. In a legal sense, an offender on probation is ordered to follow certain conditions set forth by the court, often under the supervision of a probation officer.
Differential association	In criminology, Differential Association is a theory developed by Edwin Sutherland proposing that through interaction with others, individuals learn the values, attitudes, techniques, and motives for criminal behavior.
	The Differential Association Theory is the most talked about of the Learning Theories of deviance. This theory focuses on how individuals learn to become criminals, but does not concern itself with why they become criminals.
Law enforcement	Law enforcement broadly refers to any system by which some members of society act in an organized manner to promote adherence to the law by discovering and punishing persons who violate the rules and norms governing that society. Although the term may encompass entities such as courts and prisons, it is most frequently applied to those who directly engage in patrols or surveillance to dissuade and discover criminal activity, and those who investigate crimes and apprehend offenders. Furthermore, although law enforcement may be most concerned with the prevention and punishment of crimes, organizations exist to discourage a wide variety of non-criminal violations of rules and norms, effected through the imposition of less severe consequences.
Domestic violence	Domestic violence, spousal abuse, battering, family violence, and intimate partner violence (IPV), is defined as a pattern of abusive behaviors by one partner against another in an intimate relationship such as marriage, dating, family, or cohabitation. Domestic violence, so defined, has many forms, including physical aggression or assault (hitting, kicking, biting, shoving, restraining, slapping, throwing objects), or threats thereof; sexual abuse; emotional abuse; controlling or domineering; intimidation; stalking; passive/covert abuse (e.g., neglect); and economic deprivation.

6. Policing: Issues and Challenges

CAN-SPAM Act	The CAN-SPAM Act of 2003 (15 U.S.C. 7701, et seq., Public Law No. 108-187, was S.877 of the 108th United States Congress), signed into law by President George W. Bush on December 16, 2003, establishes the United States' first national standards for the sending of commercial e-mail and requires the Federal Trade Commission (FTC) to enforce its provisions.
	The acronym CAN-SPAM derives from the bill's full name: Controlling the Assault of Non-Solicited Pornography And Marketing Act of 2003. This is also a play on the usual term for unsolicited email of this type, spam. The bill was sponsored in Congress by Senators Conrad Burns and Ron Wyden.
Joint Terrorism Task Force	A Joint Terrorism Task Force is a partnership between various U.S. law enforcement agencies that is charged with taking action against terrorism, which includes the investigation of crimes such as wire fraud and identity theft. The agencies that a Joint Terrorism Task Force comprises generally include the Federal Bureau of Investigation, other federal agencies (notably Department of Homeland Security components such as U.S. Coast Guard Investigative Service, U.S. Immigration and Customs Enforcement, U.S. Customs and Border Protection, the Transportation Security Administration, and the U.S. Secret Service as well as the Department of State's Diplomatic Security Service), state and local law enforcement, and specialized agencies, such as railroad police.
	Joint Terrorism Task Forces engage in surveillance, electronic monitoring, source development and interviews in their pursuits.
Criminal intelligence	Criminal Intelligence is information compiled, analyzed, and/or disseminated in an effort to anticipate, prevent, or monitor criminal activity.
	The United States Army Military Police defines criminal intelligence in more detail; criminal intelligence is information gathered or collated, analyzed, recorded/reported and disseminated by law enforcement agencies concerning types of crime, identified criminals and known or suspected criminal groups.
	It is particularly useful when dealing with organized crime.
Intelligence-led policing	Intelligence-led policing is a policing model that has emerged in recent years which is 'built around risk assessment and risk management.'
	Although there is no universally accepted understanding of what intelligence-led policing entails, the leading definition is that intelligence\ led\ policing is 'a strategic, future-oriented and targeted approach to crime control, focusing upon the identification, analysis and 'management' of persisting and developing 'problems' or 'risks.' In simpler terms, 'it is a model of policing in which intelligence serves as a guide to operations, rather than the reverse.

Calls for intelligence-led policing originated in the 1990s, both in Britain and in the United States. In the U.S. Mark Riebling's 1994 book Wedge - The Secret War between the FBI and CIA spotlighted the conflict between law enforcement and intelligence, and urged cops to become 'more like spies.' Intelligence-led policing gained considerable momentum globally following the September 11 terrorist attacks on the United States.

| Information sharing | The term 'information sharing' gained popularity as a result of the 9/11 Commission Hearings and its report of the United States government's lack of response to information known about the planned terrorist attack on the New York City World Trade Center prior to the event. The resulting commission report led to the enactment of several executive orders by President Bush that mandated agencies implement policies to 'share information' across organizational boundaries. In addition, an Information Sharing Environment Program Manager (PM-ISE) was appointed, tasked to implement the provisions of the Intelligence Reform and Prevention of Terrorism Act of 2004. In making recommendation toward the creation of an 'Information Sharing Environment' the 9/11 Commission based itself on the findings and recommendations made by the Markle Task Force on National Security in the Information Age. |

| Christopher Commission | The Independent Commission on the Los Angeles Police Department, informally known as the Christopher Commission, was formed in April 1991, in the wake of the Rodney King beating, by then-mayor of Los Angeles Tom Bradley. It was chaired by attorney Warren Christopher (who later became U.S. Secretary of State under President Bill Clinton). 'The commission was created to conduct 'a full and fair examination of the structure and operation of the LAPD,' including its recruitment and training practices, internal disciplinary system, and citizen complaint system.' However, with the election of Richard Riordan, these reforms were put on hold. |

| Lawsuit | A lawsuit is a civil action brought in a court of law in which a plaintiff, a party who claims to have incurred loss as a result of a defendant's actions, demands a legal or equitable remedy. The defendant is required to respond to the plaintiff's complaint. If the plaintiff is successful, judgment is in the plaintiff's favor, and a variety of court orders may be issued to enforce a right, award damages, or impose a temporary or permanent injunction to prevent an act or compel an act. |

| Fourth Amendment | The Fourth Amendment (Amendment IV) to the United States Constitution is the part of the Bill of Rights which guards against unreasonable searches and seizures, along with requiring any warrant to be judicially sanctioned and supported by probable cause. It was adopted as a response to the abuse of the writ of assistance, which is a type of general search warrant, in the American Revolution. Search and seizure (including arrest) should be limited in scope according to specific information supplied to the issuing court, usually by a law enforcement officer, who has sworn by it. The Fourth Amendment applies to the states by way of the Due Process Clause of the Fourteenth Amendment. |

6. Policing: Issues and Challenges

Due process	Due process is the legal requirement that the state must respect all of the legal rights that are owed to a person. Due process balances the power of law of the land and protects the individual person from it. When a government harms a person without following the exact course of the law, this constitutes a due-process violation, which offends against the rule of law.
Principle of legality	The principle of legality is the legal ideal that requires all law to be clear, ascertainable and non-retrospective. It requires decision makers to resolve disputes by applying legal rules that have been declared beforehand, and not to alter the legal situation retrospectively by discretionary departures from established law. It is closely related to legal formalism and the rule of law and can be traced from the writings of Feuerbach, Dicey and Montesquieu.
Community policing	Community policing is a policing strategy and philosophy based on the notion that community interaction and support can help control crime and reduce fear, with community members helping to identify suspects, detain offenders, bring problems to the attention of police, or otherwise target the social problems which give rise to a crime problem in Community policing is a philosophy that promotes organizational strategies that support the systematic use of partnerships and problem-solving techniques, which proactively address the immediate conditions that give rise to public safety issues such as crime, social disorder, and fear of crime.
	Community Policing consists of three key components:
	Community Partnerships: Collaborative partnerships between the law enforcement agency and the individuals and organizations they serve to develop solutions to problems and increase trust in police. These partnerships are forged in conjunction with other government agencies,community members and groups, human and social service providers, private businesses, and the media.
Racial profiling	Racial profiling refers to the use of an individual's race or ethnicity by law enforcement personnel as a key factor in deciding whether to engage in enforcement (e.g. make a traffic stop or arrest). The practice is controversial and is illegal in some nations.
	The concept of racial profiling has been defined in many ways, including:•'Any police-initiated action that relies on the race, ethnicity, or national origin rather than the behavior of an individual or information that leads the police to a particular individual who has been identified as being, or having been, engaged in criminal activity.' -Deborah Ramirez, Jack McDevitt, Amy Farrell for US DoJ•'Racially-biased policing occurs when law enforcement inappropriately considers race or ethnicity in deciding with whom and how to intervene in an enforcement capacity.'-Lorie Fridell, Robert Lunney, Drew Diamond and Bruce Kubu•'Using race as a key factor in deciding whether to make a traffic stop.' -General Accounting Office•'In the literature to date, there appear to be at least two clearly distinguishable definitions of the term 'racial profiling': a narrow definition and a broad definition... Under the narrow definition, racial profiling occurs when a police officer stops, questions, arrests, and/or searches someone solely on the basis of the person's race or ethnicity...

Under the broader definition, racial profiling occurs whenever police routinely use race as a factor that, along with an accumulation of other factors, causes an officer to react with suspicion and take action.'-Jim Cleary•'Use by law enforcement personnel of an individual's race or ethnicity as a factor in articulating reasonable suspicion to stop, question or arrest an individual, unless race or ethnicity is part of an identifying description of a specific suspect for a specific crime.' -Office of the Arizona Attorney GeneralIn the United States Legality

At a Federal level, racial profiling is challenged by the Fourth Amendment of the U.S. Constitution which guarantees the right to be safe from unreasonable search and seizure without probable cause and the Fourteenth Amendment which requires that all citizens be treated equally under the law.

| Deadly force | Deadly force, as defined by the United States Armed Forces, is the force which a person uses, causing-or that a person knows, or should know, would create a substantial risk of causing-death or serious bodily harm. In most jurisdictions, the use of deadly force is justified only under conditions of extreme necessity as a last resort, when all lesser means have failed or cannot reasonably be employed.

Firearms, bladed weapons, explosives, and vehicles are among those weapons the use of which is considered deadly force. |

| Ruby Ridge | Ruby Ridge was the site of a deadly confrontation and siege in northern Idaho in 1992 between Randy Weaver, his family, Weaver's friend Kevin Harris, and agents of the United States Marshals Service and Federal Bureau of Investigation. It resulted in the death of Weaver's son Sammy, his wife Vicki, and Deputy US Marshal William Francis Degan.

At the subsequent federal criminal trial of Weaver and Harris, Weaver's attorney Gerry Spence made accusations of 'criminal wrongdoing' against every agency involved in the incident: the FBI, USMS, the Bureau of Alcohol, Tobacco, Firearms and Explosives (ATF), and the United States Attorney's Office (USAO) for Idaho. |

| Taser | A Taser is an electroshock weapon that uses electrical current to disrupt voluntary control of muscles. Its manufacturer, Taser International, calls the effects 'neuromuscular incapacitation' and the devices' mechanism 'Electro-Muscular Disruption (EMD) technology'. Someone struck by a Taser experiences stimulation of his or her sensory nerves and motor nerves, resulting in strong involuntary muscle contractions. |

| Suicide | Suicide is the act of intentionally causing one's own death. Suicide is often committed out of despair, the cause of which can be attributed to a mental disorder such as depression, bipolar disorder, schizophrenia, alcoholism, or drug abuse. Stress factors such as financial difficulties or troubles with interpersonal relationships often play a significant role. |

6. Policing: Issues and Challenges

CHAPTER HIGHLIGHTS & NOTES: KEY TERMS, PEOPLE, PLACES, CONCEPTS

Suicide by cop	Suicide by cop is a suicide method in which a suicidal individual deliberately acts in a threatening way, with the goal of provoking a lethal response from a law enforcement officer or other armed individual, such as being shot to death. While the phrase is colloquial ('cop' being slang for police officer) and primarily used in the United States media, it has become the most popular name for the phenomenon. Other names include death by cop, suicide-by-police, copicide and blue suicide (a reference to the blue uniforms worn by many police officers).
Durham rule	The Durham Rule or 'product test' was adopted by the United States Court of Appeals for the District of Columbia Circuit in 1954, in the case of Durham v. U.S. (214 F.2d 862), and states that '... an accused is not criminally responsible if his unlawful act was the product of mental disease or defect'. Durham was later overturned in the case U.S. v. Brawner, 471 F.2d 969 (1972). After the 1970s, U.S. jurisdictions have tended to not recognize this argument as it places emphasis on 'mental disease or defect' and thus on testimony by psychiatrists and is argued to be somewhat ambiguous.
Criminal justice	Criminal justice is the system of practices and institutions of governments directed at upholding social control, deterring and mitigating crime, or sanctioning those who violate laws with criminal penalties and rehabilitation efforts. Those accused of crime have protections against abuse of investigatory and prosecution powers. Goals In the United States, criminal justice policy has been guided by the 1967 President's Commission on Law Enforcement and Administration of Justice, which issued a ground-breaking report 'The Challenge of Crime in a Free Society'.
National Commission on Law Observance and Enforcement	U.S. President Herbert Hoover established the Wickersham Commission, officially called the National Commission on Law Observance and Enforcement, on May 20, 1929. Former Attorney General George W. Wickersham (1858-1936) headed the 11-member group charged with identifying the causes of criminal activity and to make recommendations for appropriate public policy. During the 1928 presidential campaign Herbert Hoover supported the Eighteenth Amendment to the United States Constitution but recognized that evasion was widespread and that prohibition had fueled the growth of organized crime. Findings The Commission focused its investigations almost entirely on the widespread violations of national alcohol prohibition to study and recommend changes to the eighteenth amendment, and to observe police practices in the states.
Witness protection	Witness protection is protection of a threatened witness or any person involved in the justice system, including defendants and other clients, before, during and after a trial, usually by police.

While a witness may only require protection until the conclusion of a trial, some witnesses are provided with a new identity and may live out the rest of their lives under government protection.

Witness protection is usually required in trials against organized crime, where law enforcement sees a risk for witnesses to be intimidated by colleagues of defendants.

CHAPTER QUIZ: KEY TERMS, PEOPLE, PLACES, CONCEPTS

1. In criminology, _____ is a theory developed by Edwin Sutherland proposing that through interaction with others, individuals learn the values, attitudes, techniques, and motives for criminal behavior.

   The _____ Theory is the most talked about of the Learning Theories of deviance. This theory focuses on how individuals learn to become criminals, but does not concern itself with why they become criminals.

   a. Differential identification
   b. Disorganized offender
   c. Differential association
   d. Feminist school of criminology

2. The _____ is formally known as The City of New York Commission to Investigate Allegations of Police Corruption and the Anti-Corruption Procedures of the Police Department. Former judge Milton Mollen was appointed in July 1992 by then New York City mayor David N. Dinkins to investigate corruption in the New York City Police Department. Mollen's mandate was to examine and investigate 'the nature and extent of corruption in the Department; evaluate the departments procedures for preventing and detecting that corruption; and recommend changes and improvements to those procedures'.

   a. Homeland Security Act
   b. Mollen Commission
   c. Prison Rape Elimination Act
   d. Jessica's Law

3. _____ is the legal requirement that the state must respect all of the legal rights that are owed to a person. _____ balances the power of law of the land and protects the individual person from it. When a government harms a person without following the exact course of the law, this constitutes a due-process violation, which offends against the rule of law.

   a. Felonies
   b. Misdemeanors
   c. Due process
   d. leading questions

4. _____ is a policing strategy and philosophy based on the notion that community interaction and support can help control crime and reduce fear, with community members helping to identify suspects, detain offenders, bring problems to the attention of police, or otherwise target the social problems which give rise to a crime problem in _____ is a philosophy that promotes organizational strategies that support the systematic use of partnerships and problem-solving techniques, which proactively address the immediate conditions that give rise to public safety issues such as crime, social disorder, and fear of crime.

_____ consists of three key components:

Community Partnerships: Collaborative partnerships between the law enforcement agency and the individuals and organizations they serve to develop solutions to problems and increase trust in police. These partnerships are forged in conjunction with other government agencies,community members and groups, human and social service providers, private businesses, and the media.

   a. Problem-oriented policing
   b. Necessity
   c. Community policing
   d. Respondeat superior

5. In both crime and law, _____s (also known as bias-motivated crimes, or a race hate) occur when a perpetrator targets a victim because of his or her perceived membership in a certain social group. Examples of such groups include but are not limited to: racial group, religion, sexual orientation, ethnicity, or gender identity.

A _____ is a category used to describe bias-motivated violence: 'assault, injury, and murder on the basis of certain personal characteristics: different appearance, different color, different nationality, different language, different religion.'

'_____' generally refers to criminal acts that are seen to have been motivated by bias against one or more of the types above, or of their derivatives.

   a. Homeland Security Act
   b. Fair and Accurate Credit Transactions Act
   c. Hate crime
   d. Jessica's Law

ANSWER KEY
6. Policing: Issues and Challenges

1. c
2. b
3. c
4. c
5. c

You can take the complete Chapter Practice Test

for 6. Policing: Issues and Challenges
on all key terms, persons, places, and concepts.

Online 99 Cents

http://www.epub4670.4.23017.6.cram101.com/

Use www.Cram101.com for all your study needs

including Cram101's online interactive problem solving labs in

chemistry, statistics, mathematics, and more.

CHAPTER OUTLINE: KEY TERMS, PEOPLE, PLACES, CONCEPTS

	Crime control
	Appellate court
	Original jurisdiction
	Criminal justice
	Christopher Commission
	Hate crime
	Law enforcement
	Probable cause
	Durham rule
	Aryan Brotherhood
	Computer fraud
	Fraud
	Indictment
	Ponzi scheme
	Arraignment
	Preliminary hearing

7. The Courts

Crime control	Crime control refers to methods taken to reduce crime in a society. Penology often focuses on the use of criminal penalties as a means of deterring people from committing crimes and temporarily or permanently incapacitating those who have already committed crimes from re-offending. Crime prevention is also widely implemented in some countries, through government police and, in many cases, private policing methods such as private security and home defense.
Appellate court	An appellate court, commonly called an appeals court or court of appeals or appeal court, is any court of law that is empowered to hear an appeal of a trial court or other lower tribunal. In most jurisdictions, the court system is divided into at least three levels: the trial court, which initially hears cases and reviews evidence and testimony to determine the facts of the case; at least one intermediate appellate court; and a supreme court which primarily reviews the decisions of the intermediate courts. A jurisdiction's supreme court is that jurisdiction's highest appellate court.
Original jurisdiction	The original jurisdiction of a court is the power to hear a case for the first time, as opposed to appellate jurisdiction, when a court has the power to review a lower court's decision. France

The lowest civil court of France, the tribunal de première instance ('Court of Common Pleas'), has original jurisdiction over most civil matters except areas of specialist exclusive jurisdiction, those being mainly land estates, business and consumer matters, social security, and labor. All criminal matters may pass summarily through the lowest criminal court, the tribunal de police, but each court has both original and limited jurisdiction over certain separate levels of offences:•juge de proximité ('Magistrate Court'): petty misdemeanors and violations;•tribunal de police ('Police Court'): gross misdemeanors or summary offences (summary jurisdiction);•tribunal correctionnel ('Criminal Court'): felonies or indictable offences generally;•cour d'assises ('Court of Sessions'): capital and first-degree felonies or major indictable offences, high crimes, crimes against the State

For the administrative stream, any administrative court has original jurisdiction. |
| Criminal justice | Criminal justice is the system of practices and institutions of governments directed at upholding social control, deterring and mitigating crime, or sanctioning those who violate laws with criminal penalties and rehabilitation efforts. Those accused of crime have protections against abuse of investigatory and prosecution powers. Goals

In the United States, criminal justice policy has been guided by the 1967 President's Commission on Law Enforcement and Administration of Justice, which issued a ground-breaking report 'The Challenge of Crime in a Free Society'. |
| Christopher Commission | The Independent Commission on the Los Angeles Police Department, informally known as the Christopher Commission, was formed in April 1991, in the wake of the Rodney King beating, by then-mayor of Los Angeles Tom Bradley. It was chaired by attorney Warren Christopher (who later became U.S. Secretary of State under President Bill Clinton). |

Hate crime	In both crime and law, hate crimes (also known as bias-motivated crimes, or a race hate) occur when a perpetrator targets a victim because of his or her perceived membership in a certain social group. Examples of such groups include but are not limited to: racial group, religion, sexual orientation, ethnicity, or gender identity. A hate crime is a category used to describe bias-motivated violence: 'assault, injury, and murder on the basis of certain personal characteristics: different appearance, different color, different nationality, different language, different religion.' 'Hate crime' generally refers to criminal acts that are seen to have been motivated by bias against one or more of the types above, or of their derivatives.
Law enforcement	Law enforcement broadly refers to any system by which some members of society act in an organized manner to promote adherence to the law by discovering and punishing persons who violate the rules and norms governing that society. Although the term may encompass entities such as courts and prisons, it is most frequently applied to those who directly engage in patrols or surveillance to dissuade and discover criminal activity, and those who investigate crimes and apprehend offenders. Furthermore, although law enforcement may be most concerned with the prevention and punishment of crimes, organizations exist to discourage a wide variety of non-criminal violations of rules and norms, effected through the imposition of less severe consequences.
Probable cause	In United States criminal law, probable cause is the standard by which an officer or agent of the law has the grounds to make an arrest, to conduct a personal or property search, or to obtain a warrant for arrest, etc. when criminal charges are being considered. It is also used to refer to the standard to which a grand jury believes that a crime has been committed.
Durham rule	The Durham Rule or 'product test' was adopted by the United States Court of Appeals for the District of Columbia Circuit in 1954, in the case of Durham v. U.S. (214 F.2d 862), and states that '... an accused is not criminally responsible if his unlawful act was the product of mental disease or defect'. Durham was later overturned in the case U.S. v. Brawner, 471 F.2d 969 (1972). After the 1970s, U.S. jurisdictions have tended to not recognize this argument as it places emphasis on 'mental disease or defect' and thus on testimony by psychiatrists and is argued to be somewhat ambiguous.
Aryan Brotherhood	The Aryan Brotherhood, the AB, Alice Baker, or the One-Two, is a white supremacist prison gang and organized crime syndicate in the United States with about 20,000 members in and out of prison. According to the Federal Bureau of Investigation (FBI), the gang makes up less than 1% of the prison population, but it is responsible for up to 20% of murders in the federal prison system. The AB has focused on the economic activities typical of organized crime entities, particularly drug trafficking, extortion, inmate prostitution, and murder-for-hire.

7. The Courts

Computer fraud	Computer fraud is the use of information technology to commit fraud. In the United States, computer fraud is specifically proscribed by the Computer Fraud and Abuse Act, which provides for jail time and fines. Notable incidentsUnauthorized access at North Bay Abdulswamad Nino Macapayad, a former accounts payable clerk for North Bay Health Care Group, admitted to using her computer to access North Bay's accounting software without authorization, and in turn issued various checks payable to herself and others.
Fraud	In criminal law, a fraud is an intentional deception made for personal gain or to damage another individual; the related adjective is fraudulent. The specific legal definition varies by legal jurisdiction. Fraud is a crime, and also a civil law violation.
Indictment	An indictment in the common-law, is a formal accusation that a person has committed a crime. In jurisdictions that maintain the concept of felonies, the most serious criminal offence is a felony; jurisdictions that lack the concept of felonies often use that of an indictable offence--an offence that requires an indictment. In most common-law jurisdictions, an indictment was handed up by a grand jury, which returned a 'true bill' if it found cause to make the charge, or 'no bill' if it did not find cause.
Ponzi scheme	A Ponzi scheme is a fraudulent investment operation that pays returns to its investors from their own money or the money paid by subsequent investors, rather than from profit earned by the individual or organization running the operation. The Ponzi scheme usually entices new investors by offering higher returns than other investments, in the form of short-term returns that are either abnormally high or unusually consistent. Perpetuation of the high returns requires an ever-increasing flow of money from new investors to keep the scheme going.
Arraignment	Arraignment is a formal reading of a criminal complaint in the presence of the defendant to inform the defendant of the charges against him or her. In response to arraignment, the accused is expected to enter a plea. Acceptable pleas vary among jurisdictions, but they generally include 'guilty', 'not guilty', and the peremptory pleas (or pleas in bar) setting out reasons why a trial cannot proceed.
Preliminary hearing	Within some criminal justice systems, a preliminary hearing is a proceeding, after a criminal complaint has been filed by the prosecutor, to determine whether there is enough evidence to require a trial. In the United States, the judge must find there is probable cause that a crime was committed. In Scotland, a Preliminary Hearing is a non-evidential diet in cases to be tried before the High Court of Justiciary.

1. An _____, commonly called an appeals court or court of appeals or appeal court, is any court of law that is empowered to hear an appeal of a trial court or other lower tribunal. In most jurisdictions, the court system is divided into at least three levels: the trial court, which initially hears cases and reviews evidence and testimony to determine the facts of the case; at least one intermediate _____; and a supreme court which primarily reviews the decisions of the intermediate courts. A jurisdiction's supreme court is that jurisdiction's highest _____.

   a. United States v. Jordan
   b. Appellate court
   c. United States v. Wade
   d. Organized Crime Control Act

2. The _____, the AB, Alice Baker, or the One-Two, is a white supremacist prison gang and organized crime syndicate in the United States with about 20,000 members in and out of prison. According to the Federal Bureau of Investigation (FBI), the gang makes up less than 1% of the prison population, but it is responsible for up to 20% of murders in the federal prison system. The AB has focused on the economic activities typical of organized crime entities, particularly drug trafficking, extortion, inmate prostitution, and murder-for-hire.

   a. American Front
   b. Aryan Brotherhood
   c. Reasonable doubt
   d. Deliberation

3. In United States criminal law, _____ is the standard by which an officer or agent of the law has the grounds to make an arrest, to conduct a personal or property search, or to obtain a warrant for arrest, etc. when criminal charges are being considered. It is also used to refer to the standard to which a grand jury believes that a crime has been committed.

   a. Causation law
   b. Prima facie
   c. Reasonable doubt
   d. Probable cause

4. _____ refers to methods taken to reduce crime in a society. Penology often focuses on the use of criminal penalties as a means of deterring people from committing crimes and temporarily or permanently incapacitating those who have already committed crimes from re-offending. Crime prevention is also widely implemented in some countries, through government police and, in many cases, private policing methods such as private security and home defense.

   a. Prison rape
   b. Homeland Security Act
   c. Crime control
   d. Prison Rape Elimination Act

5. . The _____ of a court is the power to hear a case for the first time, as opposed to appellate jurisdiction, when a court has the power to review a lower court's decision. France

The lowest civil court of France, the tribunal de première instance ('Court of Common Pleas'), has _____ over most civil matters except areas of specialist exclusive jurisdiction, those being mainly land estates, business and consumer matters, social security, and labor. All criminal matters may pass summarily through the lowest criminal court, the tribunal de police, but each court has both original and limited jurisdiction over certain separate levels of offences:•juge de proximité ('Magistrate Court'): petty misdemeanors and violations;•tribunal de police ('Police Court'): gross misdemeanors or summary offences (summary jurisdiction);•tribunal correctionnel ('Criminal Court'): felonies or indictable offences generally;•cour d'assises ('Court of Sessions'): capital and first-degree felonies or major indictable offences, high crimes, crimes against the State

For the administrative stream, any administrative court has _____.

a. United States v. Jordan
b. Inkblot
c. Original jurisdiction
d. Organized Crime Control Act

ANSWER KEY
7. The Courts

1. b
2. b
3. d
4. c
5. c

You can take the complete Chapter Practice Test

for 7. The Courts
on all key terms, persons, places, and concepts.

Online 99 Cents

http://www.epub4670.4.23017.7.cram101.com/

Use www.Cram101.com for all your study needs

including Cram101's online interactive problem solving labs in

chemistry, statistics, mathematics, and more.

Aryan Brotherhood

Law enforcement

Witness protection

Court reporter

Deadly force

Expert witness

CAN-SPAM Act

District attorney

Exculpatory evidence

Model Rules of Professional Conduct

Prosecutor

Criminal lawyer

Criminal justice

Probation

Federal Rules of Criminal Procedure

Federal Rules of Evidence

Ruby Ridge

Rules of evidence

Adversarial system

Speedy trial

Speedy Trial Act

Jury selection

Peremptory challenge

Community policing

Sarbanes-Oxley Act

Scientific jury selection

Christopher Commission

Crime control

Circumstantial evidence

Direct evidence

Real evidence

Mortgage fraud

Cross-examination

Harmless error

Hate crime

Excited utterance

Hearsay

Perjury

Redirect examination

Deliberation

Hung jury

Reasonable doubt

Aryan Brotherhood	The Aryan Brotherhood, the AB, Alice Baker, or the One-Two, is a white supremacist prison gang and organized crime syndicate in the United States with about 20,000 members in and out of prison. According to the Federal Bureau of Investigation (FBI), the gang makes up less than 1% of the prison population, but it is responsible for up to 20% of murders in the federal prison system. The AB has focused on the economic activities typical of organized crime entities, particularly drug trafficking, extortion, inmate prostitution, and murder-for-hire.
Law enforcement	Law enforcement broadly refers to any system by which some members of society act in an organized manner to promote adherence to the law by discovering and punishing persons who violate the rules and norms governing that society. Although the term may encompass entities such as courts and prisons, it is most frequently applied to those who directly engage in patrols or surveillance to dissuade and discover criminal activity, and those who investigate crimes and apprehend offenders. Furthermore, although law enforcement may be most concerned with the prevention and punishment of crimes, organizations exist to discourage a wide variety of non-criminal violations of rules and norms, effected through the imposition of less severe consequences.
Witness protection	Witness protection is protection of a threatened witness or any person involved in the justice system, including defendants and other clients, before, during and after a trial, usually by police. While a witness may only require protection until the conclusion of a trial, some witnesses are provided with a new identity and may live out the rest of their lives under government protection.

Witness protection is usually required in trials against organized crime, where law enforcement sees a risk for witnesses to be intimidated by colleagues of defendants. |
| Court reporter | A court reporter, also called 'stenotype operator', 'shorthand reporter' or 'law reporter', is a person whose occupation is to transcribe spoken or recorded speech into written form, using machine shorthand or voice writing equipment to produce official transcripts of court hearings, depositions and other official proceedings. Court reporting companies primarily serve private law firms, local, state and federal government agencies and courts, trade associations, meeting planners and nonprofits. In the United States

The court reporter in some states is required to be a notary public who is authorized to administer oaths to witnesses, and who certifies that his or her transcript of the proceedings is a verbatim account of what was said. |
| Deadly force | Deadly force, as defined by the United States Armed Forces, is the force which a person uses, causing-or that a person knows, or should know, would create a substantial risk of causing-death or serious bodily harm. In most jurisdictions, the use of deadly force is justified only under conditions of extreme necessity as a last resort, when all lesser means have failed or cannot reasonably be employed. |

8. The Courtroom Work Group and the Criminal Trial

Expert witness	An expert witness, professional witness or judicial expert is a witness, who by virtue of education, training, skill, or experience, is believed to have expertise and specialised knowledge in a particular subject beyond that of the average person, sufficient that others may officially and legally rely upon the witness's specialized (scientific, technical or other) opinion about an evidence or fact issue within the scope of his expertise, referred to as the expert opinion, as an assistance to the fact-finder. Expert witnesses may also deliver expert evidence about facts from the domain of their expertise. At times, their testimony may be rebutted with a learned treatise, sometimes to the detriment of their reputations.
CAN-SPAM Act	The CAN-SPAM Act of 2003 (15 U.S.C. 7701, et seq., Public Law No. 108-187, was S.877 of the 108th United States Congress), signed into law by President George W. Bush on December 16, 2003, establishes the United States' first national standards for the sending of commercial e-mail and requires the Federal Trade Commission (FTC) to enforce its provisions. The acronym CAN-SPAM derives from the bill's full name: Controlling the Assault of Non-Solicited Pornography And Marketing Act of 2003. This is also a play on the usual term for unsolicited email of this type, spam. The bill was sponsored in Congress by Senators Conrad Burns and Ron Wyden.
District attorney	The District Attorney in many jurisdictions in the United States, is the elected or appointed official who represents the government in the prosecution of criminal offenses. The district attorney is the highest officeholder in the legal department of the jurisdiction - generally the county in the U.S. - and supervises a staff of assistant (ADA) or deputy district attorneys. Depending on the system in place, district attorneys may be appointed by the chief executive of the region or elected by the voters of the jurisdiction.
Exculpatory evidence	Exculpatory evidence is the evidence favorable to the defendant in a criminal trial, which clears or tends to clear the defendant of guilt. It is the opposite of inculpatory evidence, which tends to prove guilt. In many countries such as the United States, police or prosecutor are not required to disclose to the defendant any exculpatory evidence they possess before the defendant makes a plea (guilty or not guilty).
Model Rules of Professional Conduct	The ABA Model Rules of Professional Conduct, created by the American Bar Association (ABA), are a set of rules that prescribe baseline standards of legal ethics and professional responsibility for lawyers in the United States. They were promulgated by the ABA House of Delegates upon the recommendation of the Kutak Commission in 1983. The rules are merely recommendations, or models, (hence the name 'Model Rules') and are not themselves binding. However, having a common set of Model Rules facilitates a common discourse on legal ethics, and simplifies professional responsibility training as well as the day-to-day application of such rules.

Prosecutor	The prosecutor is the chief legal representative of the prosecution in countries with either the common law adversarial system, or the civil law inquisitorial system. The prosecution is the legal party responsible for presenting the case in a criminal trial against an individual accused of breaking the law. Common law jurisdictions

Prosecutors are typically lawyers who possess a law degree, and are recognized as legal professionals by the court in which they intend to represent the state (the society) (that is, they have been admitted to the bar). |
| Criminal lawyer | A criminal lawyer is a lawyer specializing in the defense of individuals and companies charged with criminal conduct. Criminal lawyers can be permanently employed by the various jurisdictions with criminal courts. Such lawyers are often called public defenders. |
| Criminal justice | Criminal justice is the system of practices and institutions of governments directed at upholding social control, deterring and mitigating crime, or sanctioning those who violate laws with criminal penalties and rehabilitation efforts. Those accused of crime have protections against abuse of investigatory and prosecution powers. Goals

In the United States, criminal justice policy has been guided by the 1967 President's Commission on Law Enforcement and Administration of Justice, which issued a ground-breaking report 'The Challenge of Crime in a Free Society'. |
| Probation | Probation developed from the efforts of a philanthropist, John Augustus, who looked for ways to rehabilitate the behavior of criminals. Probation literally means testing of strange behaviour or abilities. In a legal sense, an offender on probation is ordered to follow certain conditions set forth by the court, often under the supervision of a probation officer. |
| Federal Rules of Criminal Procedure | The Federal Rules of Criminal Procedure are the procedural rules that govern how federal criminal prosecutions are conducted in United States district courts, the general trial courts of the U.S. government. As such, they are the companion to the Federal Rules of Civil Procedure. The admissibility and use of evidence in criminal proceedings (as well as civil) is governed by the separate Federal Rules of Evidence. |
| Federal Rules of Evidence | The Federal Rules of Evidence is a code of evidence law governing the admission of facts by which parties in the United States federal court system may prove their cases, both civil and criminal. The Rules were enacted in 1975, with subsequent amendments.

The Rules were the product of protracted academic, legislative, and judicial examination before being formally promulgated in 1975. U.S. states are free to adopt or maintain evidence rules different from the Federal Rules, but a substantial majority have adopted codes in whole or part based on the FRE. |

8. The Courtroom Work Group and the Criminal Trial

Ruby Ridge	Ruby Ridge was the site of a deadly confrontation and siege in northern Idaho in 1992 between Randy Weaver, his family, Weaver's friend Kevin Harris, and agents of the United States Marshals Service and Federal Bureau of Investigation. It resulted in the death of Weaver's son Sammy, his wife Vicki, and Deputy US Marshal William Francis Degan.
	At the subsequent federal criminal trial of Weaver and Harris, Weaver's attorney Gerry Spence made accusations of 'criminal wrongdoing' against every agency involved in the incident: the FBI, USMS, the Bureau of Alcohol, Tobacco, Firearms and Explosives (ATF), and the United States Attorney's Office (USAO) for Idaho.
Rules of evidence	Rules of evidence govern whether, when, how, and for what purpose, proof of a legal case may be placed before a trier of fact for consideration.
	In the legal systems of Canada and the United States, the trier of fact may be a judge or a jury, depending on the purpose of the trial and the choices of the parties.
	The rules of evidence were developed over several centuries and are based upon the rules from Anglo-American common law brought to the New World by early settlers.
Adversarial system	The adversarial system is a legal system where two advocates represent their parties' positions before an impartial person or group of people, usually a jury or judge, who attempt to determine the truth of the case. As opposed to that, the inquisitorial system has a judge whose task is to investigate the case.
	The adversarial system is generally adopted in common law countries.
Speedy trial	The Speedy Trial Clause of the Sixth Amendment to the United States Constitution provides that '[i] n all criminal prosecutions, the accused shall enjoy the right to a speedy . . . trial . . . .' The Clause protects the defendant from delay between the presentation of the indictment or similar charging instrument and the beginning of trial.
Speedy Trial Act	The Speedy Trial Act of 1974, establishes time limits for completing the various stages of a federal criminal prosecution. Procedural time limits
	The Act establishes time limits for completing the various stages of a federal criminal prosecution. The information or indictment must be filed within 30 days from the date of arrest or service of the summons.
Jury selection	Jury selection are many methods used to choose the people who will serve on a trial jury. The jury pool, also known as the venire, is first selected from among the community using a reasonably random method.

Peremptory challenge	Peremptory challenge usually refers to a right in jury selection for the defense and prosecution to reject a certain number of potential jurors who appear to have an unfavorable bias without having to give any reason. Other potential jurors may be challenged for cause: i.e. by giving a reason why they might be unable to reach a fair verdict, but the challenge will be considered by the presiding judge and may be denied.

The idea behind peremptory challenges is that if both parties have contributed in the configuration of the jury, they will find its verdict more acceptable. |
| Community policing | Community policing is a policing strategy and philosophy based on the notion that community interaction and support can help control crime and reduce fear, with community members helping to identify suspects, detain offenders, bring problems to the attention of police, or otherwise target the social problems which give rise to a crime problem in Community policing is a philosophy that promotes organizational strategies that support the systematic use of partnerships and problem-solving techniques, which proactively address the immediate conditions that give rise to public safety issues such as crime, social disorder, and fear of crime.

Community Policing consists of three key components:

Community Partnerships: Collaborative partnerships between the law enforcement agency and the individuals and organizations they serve to develop solutions to problems and increase trust in police. These partnerships are forged in conjunction with other government agencies,community members and groups, human and social service providers, private businesses, and the media. |
Sarbanes-Oxley Act	The Sarbanes-Oxley Act of 2002, also known as the 'Public Company Accounting Reform and Investor Protection Act' (in the Senate) and 'Corporate and Auditing Accountability and Responsibility Act' (in the House) and more commonly called Sarbanes-Oxley, Sarbox or SOX, is a United States federal law that set new or enhanced standards for all U.S. public company boards, management and public accounting firms. S. Senator Paul Sarbanes (D-MD) and U.S. Representative Michael G. Oxley (R-OH). As a result of SOX, top management must now individually certify the accuracy of financial information.
Scientific jury selection	Scientific jury selection is the use of social science techniques and expertise to choose favorable juries during a criminal or civil trial. Scientific jury selection is used during the jury selection phase of the trial - when lawyers have the opportunity to question jurors and they and the judge choose which people will be on the jury. It almost always entails an expert's assistance in the attorney's use of peremptory challenges - the right to reject a certain number of potential jurors without stating a reason - during jury selection.
Christopher Commission	The Independent Commission on the Los Angeles Police Department, informally known as the Christopher Commission, was formed in April 1991, in the wake of the Rodney King beating, by then-mayor of Los Angeles Tom Bradley.

It was chaired by attorney Warren Christopher (who later became U.S. Secretary of State under President Bill Clinton). 'The commission was created to conduct 'a full and fair examination of the structure and operation of the LAPD,' including its recruitment and training practices, internal disciplinary system, and citizen complaint system.' However, with the election of Richard Riordan, these reforms were put on hold.

Crime control	Crime control refers to methods taken to reduce crime in a society. Penology often focuses on the use of criminal penalties as a means of deterring people from committing crimes and temporarily or permanently incapacitating those who have already committed crimes from re-offending. Crime prevention is also widely implemented in some countries, through government police and, in many cases, private policing methods such as private security and home defense.
Circumstantial evidence	Circumstantial evidence is evidence in which an inference is required to connect it to a conclusion of fact, like a fingerprint at the scene of a crime. By contrast, direct evidence supports the truth of an assertion directly-i.e., without need for any additional evidence or the intervening inference. On its own, it is the nature of circumstantial evidence for more than one explanation to still be possible.
Direct evidence	Direct evidence supports the truth of an assertion (in criminal law, an assertion of guilt or of innocence) directly, i.e., without an intervening inference. Circumstantial evidence, by contrast, consists of a fact or set of facts which, if proven, will support the creation of an inference that the matter asserted is true. For example: a witness who testifies that he saw the defendant shoot the victim gives direct evidence.
Real evidence	Real evidence, material evidence or physical evidence is any material object, introduced in a trial, intended to prove a fact in issue based on its demonstrable physical characteristics. Physical evidence can conceivably include all or part of any object. Examples Examples include the written contract, the defective part or defective product, the murder weapon, the gloves used by an alleged murderer.
Mortgage fraud	Mortgage fraud is a crime in which the intent is to materially misrepresent or omit information on a mortgage loan application to obtain a loan or to obtain a larger loan than would have been obtained had the lender or borrower known the truth. In United States federal courts, mortgage fraud is prosecuted as wire fraud, bank fraud, mail fraud and money laundering, with penalties of up to thirty years imprisonment.

Cross-examination	In law, cross-examination is the interrogation of a witness called by one's opponent. It is preceded by direct examination (in the United Kingdom, Australia, Canada, India and Pakistan known as examination-in-chief) and may be followed by a redirect (re-examination in England, Scotland, Australia, Canada, India, Hong Kong, and Pakistan). Variations by jurisdiction
	In the United States federal courts, a cross-examining attorney is typically not permitted to ask questions that do not pertain to the testimony offered during direct examination, but most state courts do permit a lawyer to cross-examine a witness on matters not raised during direct examination.
Harmless error	A harmless error is a ruling by a trial judge that, although mistaken, does not meet the burden for a losing party to reverse the original decision of the trier of fact on appeal, or to warrant a new trial. Harmless error is easiest to understand in an evidentiary context. Evidentiary errors are subject to harmless error analysis, under Federal Rule of Evidence 103(a) The general burden when arguing that evidence was improperly excluded or included is to show that the proper ruling by the trial judge may have, on the balance of probabilities, resulted in the opposite determination of fact.
Hate crime	In both crime and law, hate crimes (also known as bias-motivated crimes, or a race hate) occur when a perpetrator targets a victim because of his or her perceived membership in a certain social group. Examples of such groups include but are not limited to: racial group, religion, sexual orientation, ethnicity, or gender identity.
	A hate crime is a category used to describe bias-motivated violence: 'assault, injury, and murder on the basis of certain personal characteristics: different appearance, different color, different nationality, different language, different religion.'
	'Hate crime' generally refers to criminal acts that are seen to have been motivated by bias against one or more of the types above, or of their derivatives.
Excited utterance	An excited utterance, in the law of evidence, is a statement made by a person in response to a startling or shocking event or condition. It is an unplanned reaction to a 'startling event'. It is an exception to the hearsay rule.
Hearsay	Hearsay is information gathered by one person from another person concerning some event, condition, or thing of which the first person had no direct experience. When submitted as evidence, such statements are called hearsay evidence. As a legal term, 'hearsay' can also have the narrower meaning of the use of such information as evidence to prove the truth of what is asserted.
Perjury	Perjury, is the willful act of swearing a false oath or of falsifying an affirmation to tell the truth, whether spoken or in writing, concerning matters material to a judicial proceeding. That is, the witness falsely promises to tell the truth about matters which affect the outcome of the case.

8. The Courtroom Work Group and the Criminal Trial

Redirect examination	Redirect examination is the trial process by which the party who offered the witness has a chance to explain or otherwise qualify any damaging or accusing testimony brought out by the opponent during cross-examination. Redirect examination may question only those areas brought out on cross-examination and may not stray beyond that boundary. When a witness is presented for testimony in the U.S. judicial system, the order is 'direct' testimony, then the opposing attorney does 'cross' and then 'redirect' from the attorney first offering the witness.
Deliberation	Deliberation is a process of thoughtfully weighing options, usually prior to voting. In legal settings a jury famously uses deliberation because it is given specific options, like guilty or not guilty, along with information and arguments to evaluate. Deliberation emphasizes the use of logic and reason as opposed to power-struggle, creativity, or dialog.
Hung jury	A hung jury is a jury that cannot, by the required voting threshold, agree upon a verdict after an extended period of deliberation and is unable to change its votes. In the United States, the result is a mistrial, and the case may be retried. Some jurisdictions permit the court to give the jury a so-called Allen charge, inviting the dissenting jurors to re-examine their opinions, as a last-ditch effort to prevent the jury from hanging.
Reasonable doubt	Beyond reasonable doubt is the standard of evidence required to validate a criminal conviction in most adversarial legal systems. Generally the prosecution bears the burden of proof and is required to prove their version of events to this standard. This means that the proposition being presented by the prosecution must be proven to the extent that there could be no 'reasonable doubt' in the mind of a 'reasonable person' that the defendant is guilty.

1. The _____, the AB, Alice Baker, or the One-Two, is a white supremacist prison gang and organized crime syndicate in the United States with about 20,000 members in and out of prison. According to the Federal Bureau of Investigation (FBI), the gang makes up less than 1% of the prison population, but it is responsible for up to 20% of murders in the federal prison system. The AB has focused on the economic activities typical of organized crime entities, particularly drug trafficking, extortion, inmate prostitution, and murder-for-hire.

   a. American Front
   b. United States v. Jordan
   c. Inkblot
   d. Aryan Brotherhood

2. The _____ in many jurisdictions in the United States, is the elected or appointed official who represents the government in the prosecution of criminal offenses. The _____ is the highest officeholder in the legal department of the jurisdiction - generally the county in the U.S. - and supervises a staff of assistant (ADA) or deputy district attorneys. Depending on the system in place, district attorneys may be appointed by the chief executive of the region or elected by the voters of the jurisdiction.

   a. District attorney
   b. Homeland Security Act
   c. Fair and Accurate Credit Transactions Act
   d. Self-defense

3. _____, as defined by the United States Armed Forces, is the force which a person uses, causing-or that a person knows, or should know, would create a substantial risk of causing-death or serious bodily harm. In most jurisdictions, the use of _____ is justified only under conditions of extreme necessity as a last resort, when all lesser means have failed or cannot reasonably be employed.

   Firearms, bladed weapons, explosives, and vehicles are among those weapons the use of which is considered _____.

   a. Self-protection
   b. reasonable force
   c. Castle doctrine
   d. Deadly force

4. . _____ is a crime in which the intent is to materially misrepresent or omit information on a mortgage loan application to obtain a loan or to obtain a larger loan than would have been obtained had the lender or borrower known the truth.

   In United States federal courts, _____ is prosecuted as wire fraud, bank fraud, mail fraud and money laundering, with penalties of up to thirty years imprisonment. As the incidence of _____ has risen over the past few years, states have also begun to enact their own penalties for _____.

   a. Homeland Security Act
   b. Rules of evidence

c. Selective prosecution

d. Mortgage fraud

5. _____ is the trial process by which the party who offered the witness has a chance to explain or otherwise qualify any damaging or accusing testimony brought out by the opponent during cross-examination. _____ may question only those areas brought out on cross-examination and may not stray beyond that boundary.

When a witness is presented for testimony in the U.S. judicial system, the order is 'direct' testimony, then the opposing attorney does 'cross' and then 'redirect' from the attorney first offering the witness.

a. Homeland Security Act

b. Redirect examination

c. direct examination

d. Double Jeopardy

1. d
2. a
3. d
4. d
5. b

You can take the complete Chapter Practice Test

for 8. The Courtroom Work Group and the Criminal Trial
on all key terms, persons, places, and concepts.

Online 99 Cents

http://www.epub4670.4.23017.8.cram101.com/

Use www.Cram101.com for all your study needs

including Cram101's online interactive problem solving labs in

chemistry, statistics, mathematics, and more.

9. sentencing

CHAPTER OUTLINE: KEY TERMS, PEOPLE, PLACES, CONCEPTS

_____ Second Chance Act

_____ Incapacitation

_____ Restorative justice

_____ Computer fraud

_____ Crime control

_____ Fraud

_____ Law enforcement

_____ Comprehensive Crime Control Act

_____ Sentencing Reform Act

_____ Violent crime

_____ Federal Sentencing Guidelines

_____ Truth in sentencing

_____ Due process

_____ Due Process Clause

_____ Three-strikes laws

_____ National Crime Information Center

_____ Ponzi scheme

_____ CAN-SPAM Act

_____ Criminal justice

_____ Deadly force

_____ Violence Against Women Act

_____ | Witness protection

_____ | Job performance

_____ | Principle of legality

_____ | CrimeStat

_____ | Habeas corpus

_____ | National Association for the Advancement of Colored People

_____ | Innocence Protection Act

_____ | Combined DNA Index System

CHAPTER HIGHLIGHTS & NOTES: KEY TERMS, PEOPLE, PLACES, CONCEPTS

Second Chance Act	The Second Chance Act of 2007 (H.R. 1593), titled 'To reauthorize the grant program for reentry of offenders into the community in the Omnibus Crime Control and Safe Streets Act of 1968, to improve reentry planning and implementation, and for other purposes' was submitted to the House by Representative Danny Davis (D-IL) to amend the Omnibus Crime Control and Safe Streets Act of 1968 to reauthorize, rewrite, and expand provisions for adult and juvenile offender state and local reentry demonstration projects to provide expanded services to offenders and their families for reentry into society. H.R. 1593 was signed into law April 9, 2008. Purpose The Second Chance Act serves to reform the Omnibus Crime Control and Safe Streets Act of 1968. The purpose of the Second Chance Act is to reduce recidivism, increase public safety, and assist states and communities to address the growing population of inmates returning to communities.
Incapacitation	Incapacitation in the context of sentencing philosophy refers to the effect of a sentence in terms of positively preventing (rather than merely deterring) future offending. Imprisonment incapacitates the prisoner by physically removing them from the society against which they are deemed to have offended. Long term imprisonment with the intention to incapacitate is often used by criminal justice systems against habitual criminals who recidivate.

Restorative justice	Restorative Justice is an approach to justice that focuses on the needs of victims, offenders, as well as the involved community, instead of satisfying abstract legal principles or punishing the offender. Victims take an active role in the process, while offenders are encouraged to take responsibility for their actions, 'to repair the harm they've done--by apologizing, returning stolen money, or community service'. Restorative justice involves both victim and offender and focuses on their personal needs.
Computer fraud	Computer fraud is the use of information technology to commit fraud. In the United States, computer fraud is specifically proscribed by the Computer Fraud and Abuse Act, which provides for jail time and fines. Notable incidentsUnauthorized access at North Bay

Abdulswamad Nino Macapayad, a former accounts payable clerk for North Bay Health Care Group, admitted to using her computer to access North Bay's accounting software without authorization, and in turn issued various checks payable to herself and others. |
Crime control	Crime control refers to methods taken to reduce crime in a society. Penology often focuses on the use of criminal penalties as a means of deterring people from committing crimes and temporarily or permanently incapacitating those who have already committed crimes from re-offending. Crime prevention is also widely implemented in some countries, through government police and, in many cases, private policing methods such as private security and home defense.
Fraud	In criminal law, a fraud is an intentional deception made for personal gain or to damage another individual; the related adjective is fraudulent. The specific legal definition varies by legal jurisdiction. Fraud is a crime, and also a civil law violation.
Law enforcement	Law enforcement broadly refers to any system by which some members of society act in an organized manner to promote adherence to the law by discovering and punishing persons who violate the rules and norms governing that society. Although the term may encompass entities such as courts and prisons, it is most frequently applied to those who directly engage in patrols or surveillance to dissuade and discover criminal activity, and those who investigate crimes and apprehend offenders. Furthermore, although law enforcement may be most concerned with the prevention and punishment of crimes, organizations exist to discourage a wide variety of non-criminal violations of rules and norms, effected through the imposition of less severe consequences.
Comprehensive Crime Control Act	The Comprehensive Crime Control Act of 1984 was the first comprehensive revision of the U.S. criminal code since the early 1900s. It was signed into law by President Ronald Reagan.

9. sentencing

Sentencing Reform Act	The Sentencing Reform Act, part of the Comprehensive Crime Control Act of 1984, was a U.S. federal statute intended to increase consistency in United States federal sentencing. It established the United States Sentencing Commission. It also abolished federal parole.
Violent crime	A violent crime is a crime in which the offender uses or threatens to use violent force upon the victim. This entails both crimes in which the violent act is the objective, such as murder, as well as crimes in which violence is the means to an end, (including criminal ends) such as robbery. Violent crimes include crimes committed with weapons.
Federal Sentencing Guidelines	The Federal Sentencing Guidelines are rules that set out a uniform sentencing policy for individuals and organizations convicted of felonies and serious (Class A) misdemeanors in the United States federal courts system. The Guidelines do not apply to less serious misdemeanors. Enabling legislation
	The Guidelines are the product of the United States Sentencing Commission, which was created by the Sentencing Reform Act of 1984. The Guidelines' primary goal was to alleviate sentencing disparities that research had indicated was prevalent in the existing sentencing system, and the guidelines reform was specifically intended to provide for determinate sentencing.
Truth in sentencing	Truth in sentencing is a collection of different but related public policy stances on sentencing of those convicted of crimes in the justice system. In most contexts truth in sentencing refers to policies and legislation that aim to abolish or curb parole, so that convicts serve the period that they have been sentenced to. Truth in sentencing advocates relate such policies in terms of the public's right to know; they argue, for example, that it is deceptive to sentence an individual to 'seven to nine years', and then release the individual after he or she has served only six years.
Due process	Due process is the legal requirement that the state must respect all of the legal rights that are owed to a person. Due process balances the power of law of the land and protects the individual person from it. When a government harms a person without following the exact course of the law, this constitutes a due-process violation, which offends against the rule of law.
Due Process Clause	The Fifth and Fourteenth Amendments to the United States Constitution each contain a Due Process Clause. Due process deals with the administration of justice and thus the Due Process Clause acts as a safeguard from arbitrary denial of life, liberty, or property by the Government outside the sanction of law. The Supreme Court of the United States interprets the Clauses however more broadly because these clauses provide four protections: procedural due process (in civil and criminal proceedings), substantive due process, a prohibition against vague laws, and as the vehicle for the incorporation of the Bill of Rights.
Three-strikes laws	Three-strikes laws are statutes enacted by state governments in the United States which mandates state courts to impose harsher sentence on persons convicted of three or more serious criminal offenses. In most jurisdictions, only crimes at the felony level qualify as serious offenses.

National Crime Information Center	The National Crime Information Center is the United States' central database for tracking crime-related information. Since 1967, the National Crime Information Center has been maintained by the Federal Bureau of Investigation's Criminal Justice Information Services Division, and is interlinked with similar systems that each state maintains. Data is received from federal law enforcement agencies, state and local law enforcement agencies, as well as tribal law enforcement agencies, railroad police, and other agencies, such as state and federal motor vehicle registration and licensing authorities.
Ponzi scheme	A Ponzi scheme is a fraudulent investment operation that pays returns to its investors from their own money or the money paid by subsequent investors, rather than from profit earned by the individual or organization running the operation. The Ponzi scheme usually entices new investors by offering higher returns than other investments, in the form of short-term returns that are either abnormally high or unusually consistent. Perpetuation of the high returns requires an ever-increasing flow of money from new investors to keep the scheme going.
CAN-SPAM Act	The CAN-SPAM Act of 2003 (15 U.S.C. 7701, et seq., Public Law No. 108-187, was S.877 of the 108th United States Congress), signed into law by President George W. Bush on December 16, 2003, establishes the United States' first national standards for the sending of commercial e-mail and requires the Federal Trade Commission (FTC) to enforce its provisions. The acronym CAN-SPAM derives from the bill's full name: Controlling the Assault of Non-Solicited Pornography And Marketing Act of 2003. This is also a play on the usual term for unsolicited email of this type, spam. The bill was sponsored in Congress by Senators Conrad Burns and Ron Wyden.
Criminal justice	Criminal justice is the system of practices and institutions of governments directed at upholding social control, deterring and mitigating crime, or sanctioning those who violate laws with criminal penalties and rehabilitation efforts. Those accused of crime have protections against abuse of investigatory and prosecution powers. Goals In the United States, criminal justice policy has been guided by the 1967 President's Commission on Law Enforcement and Administration of Justice, which issued a ground-breaking report 'The Challenge of Crime in a Free Society'.
Deadly force	Deadly force, as defined by the United States Armed Forces, is the force which a person uses, causing-or that a person knows, or should know, would create a substantial risk of causing-death or serious bodily harm. In most jurisdictions, the use of deadly force is justified only under conditions of extreme necessity as a last resort, when all lesser means have failed or cannot reasonably be employed.

9. sentencing

Violence Against Women Act	The Violence Against Women Act of 1994 is a United States federal law (Title IV, sec. 40001-40703 of the Violent Crime Control and Law Enforcement Act of 1994, H.R. 3355) signed as Pub.L. 103-322 by President Bill Clinton on September 13, 1994. The Act provides $1.6 billion toward investigation and prosecution of violent crimes against women, imposes automatic and mandatory restitution on those convicted, and allows civil redress in cases prosecutors chose to leave unprosecuted. The Act also establishes the Office on Violence Against Women within the Department of Justice. Male victims of domestic violence, dating violence, sexual assault, and stalking may also be covered.
Witness protection	Witness protection is protection of a threatened witness or any person involved in the justice system, including defendants and other clients, before, during and after a trial, usually by police. While a witness may only require protection until the conclusion of a trial, some witnesses are provided with a new identity and may live out the rest of their lives under government protection. Witness protection is usually required in trials against organized crime, where law enforcement sees a risk for witnesses to be intimidated by colleagues of defendants.
Job performance	Job performance is a commonly used, yet poorly defined concept in industrial and organizational psychology, the branch of psychology that deals with the workplace. It's also part of Human Resources Management. It most commonly refers to whether a person performs their job well.
Principle of legality	The principle of legality is the legal ideal that requires all law to be clear, ascertainable and non-retrospective. It requires decision makers to resolve disputes by applying legal rules that have been declared beforehand, and not to alter the legal situation retrospectively by discretionary departures from established law. It is closely related to legal formalism and the rule of law and can be traced from the writings of Feuerbach, Dicey and Montesquieu.
CrimeStat	CrimeStat is a crime mapping software program. CrimeStat is Windows-based program that conducts spatial and statistical analysis and is designed to interface with a geographic information system (GIS). The program is developed by Ned Levine & Associates, with funding by the National Institute of Justice (NIJ), an agency of the United States Department of Justice.
Habeas corpus	A writ of is a writ (legal action) that requires a person under arrest to be brought before a judge or into court. The principle of Habeas Corpus ensures that a prisoner can be released from unlawful detention-that is, detention lacking sufficient cause or evidence. The remedy can be sought by the prisoner or by another person coming to the prisoner's aid.
National Association for the Advancement of Colored People	The National Association for the Advancement of Colored People is an African-American civil rights organization in the United States, formed in 1909. Its mission is 'to ensure the political, educational, social, and economic equality of rights of all persons and to eliminate racial hatred and racial discrimination'. Its name, retained in accordance with tradition, uses the once common term colored people.

Innocence Protection Act	In United States federal criminal law, the Innocence Protection Act is the first federal death penalty reform to be enacted. The Act seeks to ensure the fair administration of the death penalty and minimize the risk of executing innocent people. The Innocence Protection Act of 2001, introduced in the Senate as S. 486 and the House of Representatives as H.R. 912, was included as Title IV of the omnibus Justice for All Act of 2004 (H.R. 5107), signed into law on October 30, 2004 by President George W. Bush as public law no. 108-405.
Combined DNA Index System	The Combined DNA Index System is a DNA database funded by the United States Federal Bureau of Investigation (FBI). It is a computer system that stores DNA profiles created by federal, state, and local crime laboratories in the United States, with the ability to search the database to assist in the identification of suspects in crimes. Origins CODIS was an outgrowth of the Technical Working Group on DNA Analysis Methods (TWGDAM, now SWGDAM) which developed guidelines for standards of practice in the United States and Canadian crime laboratories as they began DNA testing in the late 1980s.

1. The _____ of 1994 is a United States federal law (Title IV, sec. 40001-40703 of the Violent Crime Control and Law Enforcement Act of 1994, H.R. 3355) signed as Pub.L. 103-322 by President Bill Clinton on September 13, 1994. The Act provides $1.6 billion toward investigation and prosecution of violent crimes against women, imposes automatic and mandatory restitution on those convicted, and allows civil redress in cases prosecutors chose to leave unprosecuted. The Act also establishes the Office on Violence Against Women within the Department of Justice. Male victims of domestic violence, dating violence, sexual assault, and stalking may also be covered.

    a. Homeland Security Act
    b. Violence Against Women Act
    c. Castle doctrine
    d. Self-defense

2. . The _____, part of the Comprehensive Crime Control Act of 1984, was a U.S. federal statute intended to increase consistency in United States federal sentencing. It established the United States Sentencing Commission. It also abolished federal parole.

    a. Sentencing Reform Act
    b. Bylaw enforcement officer
    c. Campus police

9. sentencing

3. _____ is the system of practices and institutions of governments directed at upholding social control, deterring and mitigating crime, or sanctioning those who violate laws with criminal penalties and rehabilitation efforts. Those accused of crime have protections against abuse of investigatory and prosecution powers. Goals

    In the United States, _____ policy has been guided by the 1967 President's Commission on Law Enforcement and Administration of Justice, which issued a ground-breaking report 'The Challenge of Crime in a Free Society'.

    a. National Criminal Justice Reference Service
    b. Homeland Security Act
    c. Criminal justice
    d. leading questions

4. In criminal law, a _____ is an intentional deception made for personal gain or to damage another individual; the related adjective is fraudulent. The specific legal definition varies by legal jurisdiction. _____ is a crime, and also a civil law violation.

    a. vandalism
    b. Larceny
    c. Fraud
    d. rustling

5. _____ is a collection of different but related public policy stances on sentencing of those convicted of crimes in the justice system. In most contexts _____ refers to policies and legislation that aim to abolish or curb parole, so that convicts serve the period that they have been sentenced to. _____ advocates relate such policies in terms of the public's right to know; they argue, for example, that it is deceptive to sentence an individual to 'seven to nine years', and then release the individual after he or she has served only six years.

    a. Homeland Security Act
    b. Fair and Accurate Credit Transactions Act
    c. Prison Rape Elimination Act
    d. Truth in sentencing

Visit Cram101.com for full Practice Exams

ANSWER KEY
9. sentencing

---

1. b
2. a
3. c
4. c
5. d

You can take the complete Chapter Practice Test

for 9. sentencing
on all key terms, persons, places, and concepts.

Online 99 Cents

http://www.epub4670.4.23017.9.cram101.com/

Use www.Cram101.com for all your study needs

including Cram101's online interactive problem solving labs in

chemistry, statistics, mathematics, and more.

CHAPTER OUTLINE: KEY TERMS, PEOPLE, PLACES, CONCEPTS

Mann Act

Probation officer

Hate crime

Community policing

Computer fraud

Fraud

Probation

Comprehensive Crime Control Act

Crime control

Criminal justice

Witness protection

Combined DNA Index System

CAN-SPAM Act

Parole officer

Sex Offender

Speedy trial

Shock probation

Recidivism

House arrest

Curfew

Second Chance Act

10. Probation, Parole, and Community Corrections

Mann Act	The White-Slave Traffic Act, better known as the Mann Act, is a United States law, passed June 25, 1910 (ch. 395, 36 Stat. 825; codified as amended at 18 U.S.C. §§ 2421-2424). Its primary stated intent was to address prostitution, 'immorality', and human trafficking; however, its ambiguous language of 'immorality' allowed selective prosecutions for many years, and was used to criminalize forms of consensual sexual behavior. It was later amended by Congress in 1978, and again in 1986 to apply only to transport for the purpose of prostitution or illegal sexual acts.
Probation officer	Parole officers and probation officers play a role in criminal justice systems by supervising offenders released from incarceration or sentenced to non-custodial sanctions such as community service. In some jurisdictions parole or probation officers are involved in presenting reports on offenders and making sentencing recommendation to courts of law. Probation and parole officers in Australia Parole officers in Canada Parole officers in Canada play a critical role at both the institutional and community levels.
Hate crime	In both crime and law, hate crimes (also known as bias-motivated crimes, or a race hate) occur when a perpetrator targets a victim because of his or her perceived membership in a certain social group. Examples of such groups include but are not limited to: racial group, religion, sexual orientation, ethnicity, or gender identity. A hate crime is a category used to describe bias-motivated violence: 'assault, injury, and murder on the basis of certain personal characteristics: different appearance, different color, different nationality, different language, different religion.' 'Hate crime' generally refers to criminal acts that are seen to have been motivated by bias against one or more of the types above, or of their derivatives.
Community policing	Community policing is a policing strategy and philosophy based on the notion that community interaction and support can help control crime and reduce fear, with community members helping to identify suspects, detain offenders, bring problems to the attention of police, or otherwise target the social problems which give rise to a crime problem in Community policing is a philosophy that promotes organizational strategies that support the systematic use of partnerships and problem-solving techniques, which proactively address the immediate conditions that give rise to public safety issues such as crime, social disorder, and fear of crime. Community Policing consists of three key components: Community Partnerships: Collaborative partnerships between the law enforcement agency and the individuals and organizations they serve to develop solutions to problems and increase trust in police. These partnerships are forged in conjunction with other government agencies,community members and groups, human and social service providers, private businesses, and the media.

Computer fraud	Computer fraud is the use of information technology to commit fraud. In the United States, computer fraud is specifically proscribed by the Computer Fraud and Abuse Act, which provides for jail time and fines. Notable incidentsUnauthorized access at North Bay Abdulswamad Nino Macapayad, a former accounts payable clerk for North Bay Health Care Group, admitted to using her computer to access North Bay's accounting software without authorization, and in turn issued various checks payable to herself and others.
Fraud	In criminal law, a fraud is an intentional deception made for personal gain or to damage another individual; the related adjective is fraudulent. The specific legal definition varies by legal jurisdiction. Fraud is a crime, and also a civil law violation.
Probation	Probation developed from the efforts of a philanthropist, John Augustus, who looked for ways to rehabilitate the behavior of criminals. Probation literally means testing of strange behaviour or abilities. In a legal sense, an offender on probation is ordered to follow certain conditions set forth by the court, often under the supervision of a probation officer.
Comprehensive Crime Control Act	The Comprehensive Crime Control Act of 1984 was the first comprehensive revision of the U.S. criminal code since the early 1900s. It was signed into law by President Ronald Reagan. Among its constituent parts and provisions were:•Armed Career Criminal Act•Sentencing Reform Act which created the United States Sentencing Commission•extension of the United States Secret Service's jurisdiction over credit card fraud and computer fraud•increased federal penalties for cultivation, possession, or transfer of marijuana•a new section in the criminal code for hostage taking•re-institution of the federal death penalty.
Crime control	Crime control refers to methods taken to reduce crime in a society. Penology often focuses on the use of criminal penalties as a means of deterring people from committing crimes and temporarily or permanently incapacitating those who have already committed crimes from re-offending. Crime prevention is also widely implemented in some countries, through government police and, in many cases, private policing methods such as private security and home defense.
Criminal justice	Criminal justice is the system of practices and institutions of governments directed at upholding social control, deterring and mitigating crime, or sanctioning those who violate laws with criminal penalties and rehabilitation efforts. Those accused of crime have protections against abuse of investigatory and prosecution powers. Goals In the United States, criminal justice policy has been guided by the 1967 President's Commission on Law Enforcement and Administration of Justice, which issued a ground-breaking report 'The Challenge of Crime in a Free Society'.
Witness protection	Witness protection is protection of a threatened witness or any person involved in the justice system, including defendants and other clients, before, during and after a trial, usually by police.

While a witness may only require protection until the conclusion of a trial, some witnesses are provided with a new identity and may live out the rest of their lives under government protection.

Witness protection is usually required in trials against organized crime, where law enforcement sees a risk for witnesses to be intimidated by colleagues of defendants.

Combined DNA Index System	The Combined DNA Index System is a DNA database funded by the United States Federal Bureau of Investigation (FBI). It is a computer system that stores DNA profiles created by federal, state, and local crime laboratories in the United States, with the ability to search the database to assist in the identification of suspects in crimes. Origins

CODIS was an outgrowth of the Technical Working Group on DNA Analysis Methods (TWGDAM, now SWGDAM) which developed guidelines for standards of practice in the United States and Canadian crime laboratories as they began DNA testing in the late 1980s. |
| CAN-SPAM Act | The CAN-SPAM Act of 2003 (15 U.S.C. 7701, et seq., Public Law No. 108-187, was S.877 of the 108th United States Congress), signed into law by President George W. Bush on December 16, 2003, establishes the United States' first national standards for the sending of commercial e-mail and requires the Federal Trade Commission (FTC) to enforce its provisions.

The acronym CAN-SPAM derives from the bill's full name: Controlling the Assault of Non-Solicited Pornography And Marketing Act of 2003. This is also a play on the usual term for unsolicited email of this type, spam. The bill was sponsored in Congress by Senators Conrad Burns and Ron Wyden. |
| Parole officer | Parole officers and probation officers play a role in criminal justice systems by supervising offenders released from incarceration or sentenced to non-custodial sanctions such as community service. In some jurisdictions parole or probation officers are involved in presenting reports on offenders and making sentencing recommendation to courts of law. Probation and parole officers in Australia

Probation and parole officers in Australia serve an active role in recommending community based supervision to Magistrates/Judges. |
| Sex Offender | A sex offender is a person who has committed a sex crime or in some instances even mere public urination. What constitutes a sex crime differs by culture and legal jurisdiction. Most jurisdictions compile their laws into sections, such as traffic, assault and sexual. |
| Speedy trial | The Speedy Trial Clause of the Sixth Amendment to the United States Constitution provides that '[i]n all criminal prosecutions, the accused shall enjoy the right to a speedy . . . trial . . . |

Shock probation	Shock probation is the policy by which a judge orders a convicted offender to prison for a short time then suspends the remainder of the sentence in favor of probation. It is hoped that the initial experience of prison will provide an effective deterrent from recidivism.
Recidivism	Recidivism is the act of a person repeating an undesirable behavior after they have either experienced negative consequences of that behavior, or have been treated or trained to extinguish that behavior. It is also used to refer to the percentage of former prisoners who are rearrested. The term is most frequently used in conjunction with criminal behavior and substance abuse .
House arrest	In justice and law, house arrest is a measure by which a person is confined by the authorities to his or her residence. Travel is usually restricted, if allowed at all. House arrest is a lenient alternative to prison time or juvenile-detention time.
Curfew	A curfew is an order specifying a time after which certain regulations apply. Examples:•An order by a government for certain persons to return home daily before a certain time. It can be imposed to maintain public order (such as those after the Northeast Blackout of 2003, the 2005 civil unrest in France, the 2010 Chile earthquake and 2011 Egyptian revolution), or suppress targeted groups.
Second Chance Act	The Second Chance Act of 2007 (H.R. 1593), titled 'To reauthorize the grant program for reentry of offenders into the community in the Omnibus Crime Control and Safe Streets Act of 1968, to improve reentry planning and implementation, and for other purposes' was submitted to the House by Representative Danny Davis (D-IL) to amend the Omnibus Crime Control and Safe Streets Act of 1968 to reauthorize, rewrite, and expand provisions for adult and juvenile offender state and local reentry demonstration projects to provide expanded services to offenders and their families for reentry into society. H.R. 1593 was signed into law April 9, 2008. Purpose The Second Chance Act serves to reform the Omnibus Crime Control and Safe Streets Act of 1968. The purpose of the Second Chance Act is to reduce recidivism, increase public safety, and assist states and communities to address the growing population of inmates returning to communities.

10. Probation, Parole, and Community Corrections

1. _____ is a policing strategy and philosophy based on the notion that community interaction and support can help control crime and reduce fear, with community members helping to identify suspects, detain offenders, bring problems to the attention of police, or otherwise target the social problems which give rise to a crime problem in _____ is a philosophy that promotes organizational strategies that support the systematic use of partnerships and problem-solving techniques, which proactively address the immediate conditions that give rise to public safety issues such as crime, social disorder, and fear of crime.

    _____ consists of three key components:

    Community Partnerships: Collaborative partnerships between the law enforcement agency and the individuals and organizations they serve to develop solutions to problems and increase trust in police. These partnerships are forged in conjunction with other government agencies,community members and groups, human and social service providers, private businesses, and the media.

    a. Problem-oriented policing
    b. Homeland Security Act
    c. Community policing
    d. Prison Rape Elimination Act

2. Parole officers and _____s play a role in criminal justice systems by supervising offenders released from incarceration or sentenced to non-custodial sanctions such as community service. In some jurisdictions parole or _____s are involved in presenting reports on offenders and making sentencing recommendation to courts of law. Probation and parole officers in Australia Parole officers in Canada

    Parole officers in Canada play a critical role at both the institutional and community levels.

    a. Probation officer
    b. Fair and Accurate Credit Transactions Act
    c. Prison Rape Elimination Act
    d. Jessica's Law

3. . The _____ of 2007 (H.R. 1593), titled 'To reauthorize the grant program for reentry of offenders into the community in the Omnibus Crime Control and Safe Streets Act of 1968, to improve reentry planning and implementation, and for other purposes' was submitted to the House by Representative Danny Davis (D-IL) to amend the Omnibus Crime Control and Safe Streets Act of 1968 to reauthorize, rewrite, and expand provisions for adult and juvenile offender state and local reentry demonstration projects to provide expanded services to offenders and their families for reentry into society. H.R. 1593 was signed into law April 9, 2008. Purpose

    The _____ serves to reform the Omnibus Crime Control and Safe Streets Act of 1968. The purpose of the _____ is to reduce recidivism, increase public safety, and assist states and communities to address the growing population of inmates returning to communities.

    a. Securities Exchange Act of 1934

b. Sherman Antitrust Act

c. Speedy Trial Act

d. Second Chance Act

4. In justice and law, _____ is a measure by which a person is confined by the authorities to his or her residence. Travel is usually restricted, if allowed at all. _____ is a lenient alternative to prison time or juvenile-detention time.

a. Chan Htoon

b. House arrest

c. Respect agenda

d. Restorative justice

5. In criminal law, a _____ is an intentional deception made for personal gain or to damage another individual; the related adjective is fraudulent. The specific legal definition varies by legal jurisdiction. _____ is a crime, and also a civil law violation.

a. vandalism

b. Fraud

c. pickpocketing

d. rustling

1. c
2. a
3. d
4. b
5. b

You can take the complete Chapter Practice Test

for 10. Probation, Parole, and Community Corrections
on all key terms, persons, places, and concepts.

Online 99 Cents

http://www.epub4670.4.23017.10.cram101.com/

Use www.Cram101.com for all your study needs

including Cram101's online interactive problem solving labs in

chemistry, statistics, mathematics, and more.

11. Prisons and Jails

	Crime control
	Hate crime
	Prison Rape Elimination Act
	Criminal justice
	Incarceration
	Community policing
	Law enforcement
	Probation
	Witness protection
	Private prison

CHAPTER HIGHLIGHTS & NOTES: KEY TERMS, PEOPLE, PLACES, CONCEPTS

Crime control	Crime control refers to methods taken to reduce crime in a society. Penology often focuses on the use of criminal penalties as a means of deterring people from committing crimes and temporarily or permanently incapacitating those who have already committed crimes from re-offending. Crime prevention is also widely implemented in some countries, through government police and, in many cases, private policing methods such as private security and home defense.
Hate crime	In both crime and law, hate crimes (also known as bias-motivated crimes, or a race hate) occur when a perpetrator targets a victim because of his or her perceived membership in a certain social group. Examples of such groups include but are not limited to: racial group, religion, sexual orientation, ethnicity, or gender identity. A hate crime is a category used to describe bias-motivated violence: 'assault, injury, and murder on the basis of certain personal characteristics: different appearance, different color, different nationality, different language, different religion.'

Prison Rape Elimination Act	The Prison Rape Elimination Act of 2003 is the first United States federal law passed dealing with the sexual assault of prisoners. The bill was signed into law on September 4, 2003. The Act was passed by both houses of the U.S. Congress and subsequently signed by President George W. Bush in a White House ceremony on September 4, 2003. The act aimed to curb prison rape through a 'zero-tolerance' policy, as well as through research and information gathering. The act called for developing national standards to prevent incidents of sexual violence in prison. It also made policies more available and obvious. By making data on prison rape more available to the prison administrators as well as making corrections facilities more accountable for incidents pertaining to sexual violence and of prison rape it would more than likely decrease the crime(s).
Criminal justice	Criminal justice is the system of practices and institutions of governments directed at upholding social control, deterring and mitigating crime, or sanctioning those who violate laws with criminal penalties and rehabilitation efforts. Those accused of crime have protections against abuse of investigatory and prosecution powers. Goals In the United States, criminal justice policy has been guided by the 1967 President's Commission on Law Enforcement and Administration of Justice, which issued a ground-breaking report 'The Challenge of Crime in a Free Society'.
Incarceration	Incarceration is the detention of a person in prison, typically as punishment for a crime (custodial sentence). People are most commonly incarcerated upon suspicion or conviction of committing a crime, and different jurisdictions have differing laws governing the function of incarceration within a larger system of justice. Incarceration serves four essential purposes with regard to criminals:•to isolate criminals to prevent them from committing more crimes•to punish criminals for committing crimes•to deter others from committing crimes•to rehabilitate criminals Incarceration rates, when measured by the United Nations, are considered distinct and separate from the imprisonment of political prisoners and others not charged with a specific crime.
Community policing	Community policing is a policing strategy and philosophy based on the notion that community interaction and support can help control crime and reduce fear, with community members helping to identify suspects, detain offenders, bring problems to the attention of police, or otherwise target the social problems which give rise to a crime problem in Community policing is a philosophy that promotes organizational strategies that support the systematic use of partnerships and problem-solving techniques, which proactively address the immediate conditions that give rise to public safety issues such as crime, social disorder, and fear of crime. Community Policing consists of three key components:

Community Partnerships: Collaborative partnerships between the law enforcement agency and the individuals and organizations they serve to develop solutions to problems and increase trust in police. These partnerships are forged in conjunction with other government agencies,community members and groups, human and social service providers, private businesses, and the media.

Law enforcement

Law enforcement broadly refers to any system by which some members of society act in an organized manner to promote adherence to the law by discovering and punishing persons who violate the rules and norms governing that society. Although the term may encompass entities such as courts and prisons, it is most frequently applied to those who directly engage in patrols or surveillance to dissuade and discover criminal activity, and those who investigate crimes and apprehend offenders. Furthermore, although law enforcement may be most concerned with the prevention and punishment of crimes, organizations exist to discourage a wide variety of non-criminal violations of rules and norms, effected through the imposition of less severe consequences.

Probation

Probation developed from the efforts of a philanthropist, John Augustus, who looked for ways to rehabilitate the behavior of criminals. Probation literally means testing of strange behaviour or abilities. In a legal sense, an offender on probation is ordered to follow certain conditions set forth by the court, often under the supervision of a probation officer.

Witness protection

Witness protection is protection of a threatened witness or any person involved in the justice system, including defendants and other clients, before, during and after a trial, usually by police. While a witness may only require protection until the conclusion of a trial, some witnesses are provided with a new identity and may live out the rest of their lives under government protection.

Witness protection is usually required in trials against organized crime, where law enforcement sees a risk for witnesses to be intimidated by colleagues of defendants.

Private prison

A private prison or for-profit prison, jail, or detention center is a place in which individuals are physically confined or interned by a third party that is contracted by a government agency. Private prison companies typically enter into contractual agreements with governments that commit prisoners and then pay a per diem or monthly rate for each prisoner confined in the facility.

Today, the privatization of prisons refers both to the takeover of existing public facilities by private operators and to the building and operation of new and additional prisons by for-profit prison companies.

1. _____ refers to methods taken to reduce crime in a society. Penology often focuses on the use of criminal penalties as a means of deterring people from committing crimes and temporarily or permanently incapacitating those who have already committed crimes from re-offending. Crime prevention is also widely implemented in some countries, through government police and, in many cases, private policing methods such as private security and home defense.

   a. Prison rape
   b. Crime control
   c. Fair and Accurate Credit Transactions Act
   d. Prison Rape Elimination Act

2. _____ broadly refers to any system by which some members of society act in an organized manner to promote adherence to the law by discovering and punishing persons who violate the rules and norms governing that society. Although the term may encompass entities such as courts and prisons, it is most frequently applied to those who directly engage in patrols or surveillance to dissuade and discover criminal activity, and those who investigate crimes and apprehend offenders. Furthermore, although _____ may be most concerned with the prevention and punishment of crimes, organizations exist to discourage a wide variety of non-criminal violations of rules and norms, effected through the imposition of less severe consequences.

   a. Law enforcement
   b. Bylaw enforcement officer
   c. Campus police
   d. Counter-terrorism

3. The _____ of 2003 is the first United States federal law passed dealing with the sexual assault of prisoners. The bill was signed into law on September 4, 2003.

   The Act was passed by both houses of the U.S. Congress and subsequently signed by President George W. Bush in a White House ceremony on September 4, 2003. The act aimed to curb prison rape through a 'zero-tolerance' policy, as well as through research and information gathering. The act called for developing national standards to prevent incidents of sexual violence in prison. It also made policies more available and obvious. By making data on prison rape more available to the prison administrators as well as making corrections facilities more accountable for incidents pertaining to sexual violence and of prison rape it would more than likely decrease the crime(s).

   a. Fair and Accurate Credit Transactions Act
   b. Homeland Security Act
   c. Prison Rape Elimination Act
   d. Jessica's Law

4. . In both crime and law, _____s (also known as bias-motivated crimes, or a race hate) occur when a perpetrator targets a victim because of his or her perceived membership in a certain social group. Examples of such groups include but are not limited to: racial group, religion, sexual orientation, ethnicity, or gender identity.

A _____ is a category used to describe bias-motivated violence: 'assault, injury, and murder on the basis of certain personal characteristics: different appearance, different color, different nationality, different language, different religion.'

'_____' generally refers to criminal acts that are seen to have been motivated by bias against one or more of the types above, or of their derivatives.

a. Homeland Security Act
b. Fair and Accurate Credit Transactions Act
c. Hate crime
d. Jessica's Law

5. _____ is the system of practices and institutions of governments directed at upholding social control, deterring and mitigating crime, or sanctioning those who violate laws with criminal penalties and rehabilitation efforts. Those accused of crime have protections against abuse of investigatory and prosecution powers. Goals

In the United States, _____ policy has been guided by the 1967 President's Commission on Law Enforcement and Administration of Justice, which issued a ground-breaking report 'The Challenge of Crime in a Free Society'.

a. National Criminal Justice Reference Service
b. Homeland Security Act
c. Fair and Accurate Credit Transactions Act
d. Criminal justice

Visit Cram101.com for full Practice Exams

ANSWER KEY
11. Prisons and Jails

---

1. b
2. a
3. c
4. c
5. d

You can take the complete Chapter Practice Test

for 11. Prisons and Jails
on all key terms, persons, places, and concepts.

Online 99 Cents

http://www.epub4670.4.23017.11.cram101.com/

Use www.Cram101.com for all your study needs

including Cram101's online interactive problem solving labs in

chemistry, statistics, mathematics, and more.

CHAPTER OUTLINE: KEY TERMS, PEOPLE, PLACES, CONCEPTS

	Law enforcement
	Criminal justice
	Hate crime
	Community policing
	Probation
	Prison Rape Elimination Act
	Sex Offender
	Witness protection
	Staffing
	Aryan Brotherhood
	Mexican Mafia
	Texas Syndicate
	Christopher Commission
	Balancing test
	Computer fraud
	Fraud
	Habeas corpus
	Due process
	Second Chance Act
	Prison Litigation Reform Act

12. Prison Life

Law enforcement	Law enforcement broadly refers to any system by which some members of society act in an organized manner to promote adherence to the law by discovering and punishing persons who violate the rules and norms governing that society. Although the term may encompass entities such as courts and prisons, it is most frequently applied to those who directly engage in patrols or surveillance to dissuade and discover criminal activity, and those who investigate crimes and apprehend offenders. Furthermore, although law enforcement may be most concerned with the prevention and punishment of crimes, organizations exist to discourage a wide variety of non-criminal violations of rules and norms, effected through the imposition of less severe consequences.
Criminal justice	Criminal justice is the system of practices and institutions of governments directed at upholding social control, deterring and mitigating crime, or sanctioning those who violate laws with criminal penalties and rehabilitation efforts. Those accused of crime have protections against abuse of investigatory and prosecution powers. Goals

In the United States, criminal justice policy has been guided by the 1967 President's Commission on Law Enforcement and Administration of Justice, which issued a ground-breaking report 'The Challenge of Crime in a Free Society'. |
| Hate crime | In both crime and law, hate crimes (also known as bias-motivated crimes, or a race hate) occur when a perpetrator targets a victim because of his or her perceived membership in a certain social group. Examples of such groups include but are not limited to: racial group, religion, sexual orientation, ethnicity, or gender identity.

A hate crime is a category used to describe bias-motivated violence: 'assault, injury, and murder on the basis of certain personal characteristics: different appearance, different color, different nationality, different language, different religion.'

'Hate crime' generally refers to criminal acts that are seen to have been motivated by bias against one or more of the types above, or of their derivatives. |
| Community policing | Community policing is a policing strategy and philosophy based on the notion that community interaction and support can help control crime and reduce fear, with community members helping to identify suspects, detain offenders, bring problems to the attention of police, or otherwise target the social problems which give rise to a crime problem in Community policing is a philosophy that promotes organizational strategies that support the systematic use of partnerships and problem-solving techniques, which proactively address the immediate conditions that give rise to public safety issues such as crime, social disorder, and fear of crime.

Community Policing consists of three key components: |

	Community Partnerships: Collaborative partnerships between the law enforcement agency and the individuals and organizations they serve to develop solutions to problems and increase trust in police. These partnerships are forged in conjunction with other government agencies,community members and groups, human and social service providers, private businesses, and the media.
Probation	Probation developed from the efforts of a philanthropist, John Augustus, who looked for ways to rehabilitate the behavior of criminals. Probation literally means testing of strange behaviour or abilities. In a legal sense, an offender on probation is ordered to follow certain conditions set forth by the court, often under the supervision of a probation officer.
Prison Rape Elimination Act	The Prison Rape Elimination Act of 2003 is the first United States federal law passed dealing with the sexual assault of prisoners. The bill was signed into law on September 4, 2003.
	The Act was passed by both houses of the U.S. Congress and subsequently signed by President George W. Bush in a White House ceremony on September 4, 2003. The act aimed to curb prison rape through a 'zero-tolerance' policy, as well as through research and information gathering. The act called for developing national standards to prevent incidents of sexual violence in prison. It also made policies more available and obvious. By making data on prison rape more available to the prison administrators as well as making corrections facilities more accountable for incidents pertaining to sexual violence and of prison rape it would more than likely decrease the crime(s).
Sex Offender	A sex offender is a person who has committed a sex crime or in some instances even mere public urination. What constitutes a sex crime differs by culture and legal jurisdiction. Most jurisdictions compile their laws into sections, such as traffic, assault and sexual.
Witness protection	Witness protection is protection of a threatened witness or any person involved in the justice system, including defendants and other clients, before, during and after a trial, usually by police. While a witness may only require protection until the conclusion of a trial, some witnesses are provided with a new identity and may live out the rest of their lives under government protection.
	Witness protection is usually required in trials against organized crime, where law enforcement sees a risk for witnesses to be intimidated by colleagues of defendants.
Staffing	Staffing is a term used in the sphere of employment. It has been applied to more than one aspect of the working environment.
	Staffing has been defined as follows by Heneman and Judge in Staffing Organisation (5th Edn 2005)'

12. Prison Life

Aryan Brotherhood	The Aryan Brotherhood, the AB, Alice Baker, or the One-Two, is a white supremacist prison gang and organized crime syndicate in the United States with about 20,000 members in and out of prison. According to the Federal Bureau of Investigation (FBI), the gang makes up less than 1% of the prison population, but it is responsible for up to 20% of murders in the federal prison system. The AB has focused on the economic activities typical of organized crime entities, particularly drug trafficking, extortion, inmate prostitution, and murder-for-hire.
Mexican Mafia	The Mexican Mafia, is a Mexican American highly-organized, ruthless crime organization in the United States. Despite its name, the Mexican Mafia did not originate in Mexico and is entirely a U.S. criminal prison organization. Sureños, including MS-13 and Florencia 13, use the number 13 to show allegiance to the Mexican Mafia.
Texas Syndicate	The Texas Syndicate is a mostly Texas-based prison gang that includes Hispanic and at one time, White (non-Hispanic) members. The Texas Syndicate, unlike La Eme or Nuestra Familia, has been more associated or allied with Mexican immigrant prisoners, known as 'border brothers', while La Eme and the NF tend to be more composed of US-born/raised Hispanics. It was established in the 1970s at Folsom Prison in California in direct response to the other California prison gangs (notably the Aryan Brotherhood and Mexican Mafia), which were attempting to prey on native Texas inmates.
Christopher Commission	The Independent Commission on the Los Angeles Police Department, informally known as the Christopher Commission, was formed in April 1991, in the wake of the Rodney King beating, by then-mayor of Los Angeles Tom Bradley. It was chaired by attorney Warren Christopher (who later became U.S. Secretary of State under President Bill Clinton). 'The commission was created to conduct 'a full and fair examination of the structure and operation of the LAPD,' including its recruitment and training practices, internal disciplinary system, and citizen complaint system.' However, with the election of Richard Riordan, these reforms were put on hold.
Balancing test	A balancing test is any judicial test in which the jurists weigh the importance of multiple factors in a legal case. Proponents of such tests argue that they allow a deeper consideration of complex issues than a bright line rule can allow. But critics say that such tests can be used to justify any conclusion which the judge might arbitrarily decide upon.
Computer fraud	Computer fraud is the use of information technology to commit fraud. In the United States, computer fraud is specifically proscribed by the Computer Fraud and Abuse Act, which provides for jail time and fines. Notable incidentsUnauthorized access at North Bay Abdulswamad Nino Macapayad, a former accounts payable clerk for North Bay Health Care Group, admitted to using her computer to access North Bay's accounting software without authorization, and in turn issued various checks payable to herself and others.

Fraud	In criminal law, a fraud is an intentional deception made for personal gain or to damage another individual; the related adjective is fraudulent. The specific legal definition varies by legal jurisdiction. Fraud is a crime, and also a civil law violation.
Habeas corpus	A writ of is a writ (legal action) that requires a person under arrest to be brought before a judge or into court. The principle of Habeas Corpus ensures that a prisoner can be released from unlawful detention-that is, detention lacking sufficient cause or evidence. The remedy can be sought by the prisoner or by another person coming to the prisoner's aid.
Due process	Due process is the legal requirement that the state must respect all of the legal rights that are owed to a person. Due process balances the power of law of the land and protects the individual person from it. When a government harms a person without following the exact course of the law, this constitutes a due-process violation, which offends against the rule of law.
Second Chance Act	The Second Chance Act of 2007 (H.R. 1593), titled 'To reauthorize the grant program for reentry of offenders into the community in the Omnibus Crime Control and Safe Streets Act of 1968, to improve reentry planning and implementation, and for other purposes' was submitted to the House by Representative Danny Davis (D-IL) to amend the Omnibus Crime Control and Safe Streets Act of 1968 to reauthorize, rewrite, and expand provisions for adult and juvenile offender state and local reentry demonstration projects to provide expanded services to offenders and their families for reentry into society. H.R. 1593 was signed into law April 9, 2008. Purpose The Second Chance Act serves to reform the Omnibus Crime Control and Safe Streets Act of 1968. The purpose of the Second Chance Act is to reduce recidivism, increase public safety, and assist states and communities to address the growing population of inmates returning to communities.
Prison Litigation Reform Act	The Prison Litigation Reform Act is a U.S. federal law that was enacted in 1996. Congress enacted Prison Litigation Reform Act in response to a significant increase in prisoner litigation in the federal courts; the Prison Litigation Reform Act was designed to decrease the incidence of legislation within the court system. For the preceding 20 - 30 years, many prisons and jails in the United States had been enjoined to make certain changes based on findings that the conditions of these institutions violated the constitutional rights of inmates (in particular, freedom from cruel and unusual punishment or the right to due process). Many of these injunctions came as a result of consent decrees entered into between inmates and prison officials and endorsed by federal courts, so that relief was not necessarily tied to violations found.

12. Prison Life

1. _____ is a policing strategy and philosophy based on the notion that community interaction and support can help control crime and reduce fear, with community members helping to identify suspects, detain offenders, bring problems to the attention of police, or otherwise target the social problems which give rise to a crime problem in _____ is a philosophy that promotes organizational strategies that support the systematic use of partnerships and problem-solving techniques, which proactively address the immediate conditions that give rise to public safety issues such as crime, social disorder, and fear of crime.

   _____ consists of three key components:

   Community Partnerships: Collaborative partnerships between the law enforcement agency and the individuals and organizations they serve to develop solutions to problems and increase trust in police. These partnerships are forged in conjunction with other government agencies,community members and groups, human and social service providers, private businesses, and the media.

   a. Problem-oriented policing
   b. Homeland Security Act
   c. Fair and Accurate Credit Transactions Act
   d. Community policing

2. The _____ is a mostly Texas-based prison gang that includes Hispanic and at one time, White (non-Hispanic) members. The _____, unlike La Eme or Nuestra Familia, has been more associated or allied with Mexican immigrant prisoners, known as 'border brothers', while La Eme and the NF tend to be more composed of US-born/raised Hispanics.

   It was established in the 1970s at Folsom Prison in California in direct response to the other California prison gangs (notably the Aryan Brotherhood and Mexican Mafia), which were attempting to prey on native Texas inmates.

   a. Homeland Security Act
   b. Derby sex gang
   c. Fair and Accurate Credit Transactions Act
   d. Texas Syndicate

3. The _____, is a Mexican American highly-organized, ruthless crime organization in the United States. Despite its name, the _____ did not originate in Mexico and is entirely a U.S. criminal prison organization. Sureños, including MS-13 and Florencia 13, use the number 13 to show allegiance to the _____.

   a. Homeland Security Act
   b. Derby sex gang
   c. Fair and Accurate Credit Transactions Act
   d. Mexican Mafia

4. . _____ is the legal requirement that the state must respect all of the legal rights that are owed to a person. _____ balances the power of law of the land and protects the individual person from it. When a government harms a person without following the exact course of the law, this constitutes a due-process violation, which offends against the rule of law.

a. Felonies
b. Due process
c. restraining orders
d. leading questions

5. In both crime and law, _____s (also known as bias-motivated crimes, or a race hate) occur when a perpetrator targets a victim because of his or her perceived membership in a certain social group. Examples of such groups include but are not limited to: racial group, religion, sexual orientation, ethnicity, or gender identity.

A _____ is a category used to describe bias-motivated violence: 'assault, injury, and murder on the basis of certain personal characteristics: different appearance, different color, different nationality, different language, different religion.'

'_____' generally refers to criminal acts that are seen to have been motivated by bias against one or more of the types above, or of their derivatives.

a. Homeland Security Act
b. Fair and Accurate Credit Transactions Act
c. Prison Rape Elimination Act
d. Hate crime

1. d
2. d
3. d
4. b
5. d

You can take the complete Chapter Practice Test

for 12. Prison Life
on all key terms, persons, places, and concepts.

Online 99 Cents

http://www.epub4670.4.23017.12.cram101.com/

Use www.Cram101.com for all your study needs

including Cram101's online interactive problem solving labs in

chemistry, statistics, mathematics, and more.

13. Juvenile Justice

Juvenile court

Parens patriae

Status offense

Crime control

AMBER alert

Computer fraud

Fraud

Concurrent jurisdiction

Original jurisdiction

Insanity defense

Ponzi scheme

Preliminary hearing

Digital evidence

CAN-SPAM Act

Community policing

Due process

Juvenile court	A juvenile court is a tribunal having special authority to try and pass judgments for crimes committed by children or adolescents who have not attained the age of majority. In most modern legal systems, crimes committed by children and minors are treated differently to the same crimes committed by adults.
	Severe offenses, such as murder and gang-related acts, in **44** states of the USA are treated the same as crimes committed by adults.
Parens patriae	Parens patriae is Latin for 'parent of the nation.' In law, it refers to the public policy power of the state to intervene against an abusive or negligent parent, legal guardian or informal caretaker, and to act as the parent of any child or individual who is in need of protection. For example, some children, incapacitated individuals, and disabled individuals lack parents who are able and willing to render adequate care, requiring state intervention.
	In U.S. litigation, parens patriae can be invoked by the state to create its standing to sue; the state declares itself to be suing on behalf of its people.
Status offense	Two common definitions of a status offense or status crime are
	1. A status offense is an action that is prohibited only to a certain class of people, and most often applied to offenses only committed by minors.
	2. In the United States, the term status offense refers to an offense such as a traffic violation where motive is not a consideration in determining guilt. In the United Kingdom and Europe, this type of status offense may be termed a regulatory offense.
Crime control	Crime control refers to methods taken to reduce crime in a society. Penology often focuses on the use of criminal penalties as a means of deterring people from committing crimes and temporarily or permanently incapacitating those who have already committed crimes from re-offending. Crime prevention is also widely implemented in some countries, through government police and, in many cases, private policing methods such as private security and home defense.
AMBER alert	An AMBER Alert is a child abduction alert system originating in 1996, now employed in 9 countries. AMBER is officially a backronym for America's Missing: Broadcasting Emergency Response a 9-year-old abducted and murdered in Arlington, Texas in 1996. Alternate regional alert names were once used; in Georgia, 'Levi's Call' ; in Hawaii, 'Maile Amber Alert' (after Maile Gilbert); and Arkansas, 'Morgan Nick Amber Alert' (in memory of Morgan Chauntel Nick).
	AMBER Alerts are distributed via commercial radio stations, Internet radio, satellite radio, television stations, and cable TV by the Emergency Alert System and NOAA Weather Radio (where they are termed 'Child Abduction Emergency' or 'Amber Alerts').

13. Juvenile Justice

Computer fraud	Computer fraud is the use of information technology to commit fraud. In the United States, computer fraud is specifically proscribed by the Computer Fraud and Abuse Act, which provides for jail time and fines. Notable incidentsUnauthorized access at North Bay Abdulswamad Nino Macapayad, a former accounts payable clerk for North Bay Health Care Group, admitted to using her computer to access North Bay's accounting software without authorization, and in turn issued various checks payable to herself and others.
Fraud	In criminal law, a fraud is an intentional deception made for personal gain or to damage another individual; the related adjective is fraudulent. The specific legal definition varies by legal jurisdiction. Fraud is a crime, and also a civil law violation.
Concurrent jurisdiction	Concurrent jurisdiction exists where two or more courts from different systems simultaneously have jurisdiction over a specific case. This situation leads to forum shopping, as parties will try to have their civil or criminal case heard in the court that they perceive will be most favorable to them. United States In the United States, concurrent jurisdiction exists to the extent that the United States Constitution permits federal courts to hear actions that can also be heard by state courts.
Original jurisdiction	The original jurisdiction of a court is the power to hear a case for the first time, as opposed to appellate jurisdiction, when a court has the power to review a lower court's decision. France The lowest civil court of France, the tribunal de première instance ('Court of Common Pleas'), has original jurisdiction over most civil matters except areas of specialist exclusive jurisdiction, those being mainly land estates, business and consumer matters, social security, and labor. All criminal matters may pass summarily through the lowest criminal court, the tribunal de police, but each court has both original and limited jurisdiction over certain separate levels of offences:•juge de proximité ('Magistrate Court'): petty misdemeanors and violations;•tribunal de police ('Police Court'): gross misdemeanors or summary offences (summary jurisdiction);•tribunal correctionnel ('Criminal Court'): felonies or indictable offences generally;•cour d'assises ('Court of Sessions'): capital and first-degree felonies or major indictable offences, high crimes, crimes against the State For the administrative stream, any administrative court has original jurisdiction.
Insanity defense	In criminal trials, the insanity defense is where the defendant claims that he or she was not responsible for his or her actions due to mental health problems (psychiatric illness or mental handicap). The exemption of the insane from full criminal punishment dates back to at least the Code of Hammurabi. There are different definitions of legal insanity, such as the M'Naghten Rules, the Durham Rule, the American Legal Institute definition, and various miscellaneous provisions .

Ponzi scheme	A Ponzi scheme is a fraudulent investment operation that pays returns to its investors from their own money or the money paid by subsequent investors, rather than from profit earned by the individual or organization running the operation. The Ponzi scheme usually entices new investors by offering higher returns than other investments, in the form of short-term returns that are either abnormally high or unusually consistent. Perpetuation of the high returns requires an ever-increasing flow of money from new investors to keep the scheme going.
Preliminary hearing	Within some criminal justice systems, a preliminary hearing is a proceeding, after a criminal complaint has been filed by the prosecutor, to determine whether there is enough evidence to require a trial. In the United States, the judge must find there is probable cause that a crime was committed. In Scotland, a Preliminary Hearing is a non-evidential diet in cases to be tried before the High Court of Justiciary.
Digital evidence	Digital evidence is any probative information stored or transmitted in digital form that a party to a court case may use at trial. Before accepting digital evidence a court will determine if the evidence is relevant, whether it is authentic, if it is hearsay and whether a copy is acceptable or the original is required. The use of digital evidence has increased in the past few decades as courts have allowed the use of e-mails, digital photographs, ATM transaction logs, word processing documents, instant message histories, files saved from accounting programs, spreadsheets, internet browser histories, databases, the contents of computer memory, computer backups, computer printouts, Global Positioning System tracks, logs from a hotel's electronic door locks, and digital video or audio files.
CAN-SPAM Act	The CAN-SPAM Act of 2003 (15 U.S.C. 7701, et seq., Public Law No. 108-187, was S.877 of the 108th United States Congress), signed into law by President George W. Bush on December 16, 2003, establishes the United States' first national standards for the sending of commercial e-mail and requires the Federal Trade Commission (FTC) to enforce its provisions. The acronym CAN-SPAM derives from the bill's full name: Controlling the Assault of Non-Solicited Pornography And Marketing Act of 2003. This is also a play on the usual term for unsolicited email of this type, spam. The bill was sponsored in Congress by Senators Conrad Burns and Ron Wyden.

13. Juvenile Justice

Community policing	Community policing is a policing strategy and philosophy based on the notion that community interaction and support can help control crime and reduce fear, with community members helping to identify suspects, detain offenders, bring problems to the attention of police, or otherwise target the social problems which give rise to a crime problem in Community policing is a philosophy that promotes organizational strategies that support the systematic use of partnerships and problem-solving techniques, which proactively address the immediate conditions that give rise to public safety issues such as crime, social disorder, and fear of crime. Community Policing consists of three key components: Community Partnerships: Collaborative partnerships between the law enforcement agency and the individuals and organizations they serve to develop solutions to problems and increase trust in police. These partnerships are forged in conjunction with other government agencies,community members and groups, human and social service providers, private businesses, and the media.
Due process	Due process is the legal requirement that the state must respect all of the legal rights that are owed to a person. Due process balances the power of law of the land and protects the individual person from it. When a government harms a person without following the exact course of the law, this constitutes a due-process violation, which offends against the rule of law.

1. Within some criminal justice systems, a _____ is a proceeding, after a criminal complaint has been filed by the prosecutor, to determine whether there is enough evidence to require a trial. In the United States, the judge must find there is probable cause that a crime was committed.

   In Scotland, a _____ is a non-evidential diet in cases to be tried before the High Court of Justiciary.

   a. Preliminary hearing
   b. Black money scam
   c. Fair and Accurate Credit Transactions Act
   d. UCL Jill Dando Institute

2. . _____ exists where two or more courts from different systems simultaneously have jurisdiction over a specific case. This situation leads to forum shopping, as parties will try to have their civil or criminal case heard in the court that they perceive will be most favorable to them. United States

In the United States, _____ exists to the extent that the United States Constitution permits federal courts to hear actions that can also be heard by state courts.

a. Homeland Security Act
b. Concurrent jurisdiction
c. pickpocketing
d. rustling

3. _____ is the use of information technology to commit fraud. In the United States, _____ is specifically proscribed by the _____ and Abuse Act, which provides for jail time and fines. Notable incidentsUnauthorized access at North Bay

Abdulswamad Nino Macapayad, a former accounts payable clerk for North Bay Health Care Group, admitted to using her computer to access North Bay's accounting software without authorization, and in turn issued various checks payable to herself and others.

a. Homeland Security Act
b. Fair and Accurate Credit Transactions Act
c. Computer fraud
d. Jessica's Law

4. In criminal law, a _____ is an intentional deception made for personal gain or to damage another individual; the related adjective is fraudulent. The specific legal definition varies by legal jurisdiction. _____ is a crime, and also a civil law violation.

a. Fraud
b. Larceny
c. pickpocketing
d. rustling

5. A _____ is a tribunal having special authority to try and pass judgments for crimes committed by children or adolescents who have not attained the age of majority. In most modern legal systems, crimes committed by children and minors are treated differently to the same crimes committed by adults.

Severe offenses, such as murder and gang-related acts, in 44 states of the USA are treated the same as crimes committed by adults.

a. Homeland Security Act
b. Juvenile court
c. Prison Rape Elimination Act
d. Jessica's Law

1. a
2. b
3. c
4. a
5. b

You can take the complete Chapter Practice Test

for 13. Juvenile Justice
on all key terms, persons, places, and concepts.

Online 99 Cents

http://www.epub4670.4.23017.13.cram101.com/

Use www.Cram101.com for all your study needs

including Cram101's online interactive problem solving labs in

chemistry, statistics, mathematics, and more.

Other Cram101 e-Books and Tests

Want More?
Cram101.com...

Cram101.com provides the outlines and highlights of your
textbooks, just like this e-StudyGuide, but also gives you the
PRACTICE TESTS, and other exclusive study tools for all of your
textbooks.

Learn More. *Just click*
http://www.cram101.com/

Other Cram101 e-Books and Tests

CPSIA information can be obtained at www.ICGtesting.com
Printed in the USA
BVOW05s0917050214

344025BV00001B/67/P

9 781490 244037